HORSE TACK
BIBLE

CAROLYN HENDERSON

A DAVID & CHARLES BOOK
Copyright © David & Charles Limited 2008, 2009

David & Charles is an F+W Media, Inc. company
4700 East Galbraith Road
Cincinnati, OH 45236

First published in the UK and USA in 2008
This paperback edition first published in the UK in 2009

Text copyright © Carolyn Henderson 2008, 2009
All photographs copyright © John Henderson 2008, 2009 except the following
pages: 16 (top) copyright © Heather Moffett; 54, 70 and 74 (top) copyright ©
Myler Bits; 73 (top) and 100 (right) copyright © Parelli; 79, 136 (top) and 166
(middle) copyright © Equilibrium Products; 113 copyright © Barnsby/ Free
Training Systems; 122 copyright © David & Charles; 128 and 157 copyright ©
Belstane Marketing; 146 (bottom) copyright © Kentaur; 156 (bottom) copyright
© Horseware Ireland; 165 (top left, top right and middle) copyright © Snuggy
Hoods; 165 (bottom) copyright © National Sweet Itch Helpline; 169 (top)
copyright © Weaver Equine; 170 and 171 copyright © V-Bandz.

Carolyn Henderson has asserted her right to be identified as author of this work
in accordance with the Copyright, Designs and Patents Act, 1988.

A catalogue record for this book is available from the British Library.

ISBN-13: 978-0-7153-2879-8 paperback
ISBN-10: 0-7153-2879-4 paperback

Printed in Singapore by KHL Printing Co. Pte Ltd
for David & Charles
Brunel House   Newton Abbot   Devon

Commissioning Editor: Jane Trollope
Desk Editor: Emily Rae
Art Editor: Charly Bailey
Senior Designer: Jodie Lystor
Production Controller: Beverley Richardson
Photographer: John Henderson

Visit our website at www.davidandcharles.co.uk

David & Charles books are available from all good bookshops; alternatively you
can contact our Orderline on 0870 9908222 or write to us at FREEPOST EX2
110, D&C Direct, Newton Abbot, TQ12 4ZZ (no stamp required UK only); US
customers call 800-289-0963 and Canadian customers call 800-840-5220.

INTRODUCTION

Choosing the right tack and equipment helps you make the most of your partnership with your horse. It plays a vital role in everything from ensuring his and your comfort to helping you achieve the best communication and performance, whether you enjoy competing or ride purely for pleasure. But because there are so many products and designs available, it can be a confusing subject, which is where this book comes in.

Although small changes can sometimes make a big difference, it's important to look at the overall picture of how you keep and ride your horse. For instance, although a different bit may give you better communication with a horse who pulls or is excitable, you also need to think about whether your riding technique or feeding regime may be contributing to problems. A change of tack will often help, but combine this with advice from a good trainer and you'll see even more improvement.

This book will help whether you're buying tack and equipment for the first time or are an experienced rider looking to replace or update items. There are many new ideas, though 'new' does not automatically mean 'better'. So although you'll find some of the most up-to-date ideas, you'll also find classics that are as valuable to today's horses and riders as they were to previous generations.

Information on fitting and adjustment is also aimed at riders of all levels. Look at

any equestrian magazine or go to any big competition and you'll see a surprising amount of badly fitting tack. It's a subject that the equestrian disciplines' governing bodies, national and international, are looking at as part of their holistic approach, so don't take your tack for granted.

Successful professionals choose the tack and equipment they use with as much care as they plan their horses' feeding and schooling regimes. What works for a showing rider may not work for, say, a Western or endurance specialist, but that's part of the challenge. At the same time, they have common priorities and principles.

Above all, look at and listen to your horse. Study his mouth conformation to help you find the right bit, and make sure he has regular dental checks; check the fit of your saddle regularly; watch his reactions when you fasten the girth; ask yourself if the reason he tries to lean on the bit is that you're setting your hands against him. He can't tell you if he's comfortable or uncomfortable, but he'll definitely show you.

There will be times when you need advice from a qualified professional such as a vet, equine dental technician or saddle fitter. This book isn't meant to replace the expertise of someone who can see you and your horse in action, but as an accompaniment to it. Put everything together and hopefully, you'll be tacked up for success.

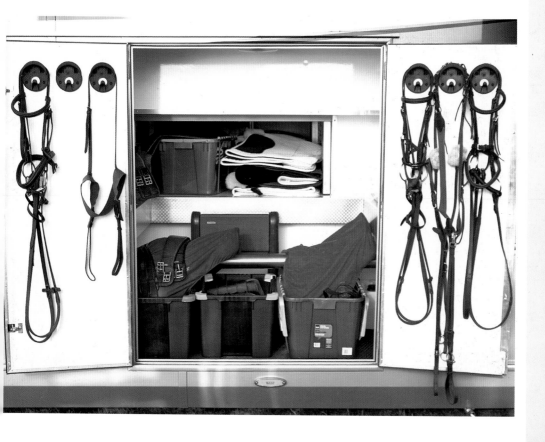

1

SADDLES

CONTENTS

FIT FOR THE JOB

Whatever type of saddle you choose (see pages 12–13) it's vital that it fits your horse, as incorrect fit will lead to discomfort, poor performance and even long-term damage to muscles and ligaments. A knowledgeable saddle fitter should be part of your back-up team, but you need to understand general fitting guidelines and be able to assess your horse and his saddle regularly.

Basic checks are common sense, not rocket science. Start by having your saddle professionally fitted and then check the fit every month, and whenever you suspect a problem, because horses change shape as they gain or lose weight and/or musculature. That way, you can call in your expert before problems arise.

To assess saddle fit, you need an observant but not necessarily horsey helper or, if you prefer to take the observer role, a rider roughly the same height, shape and weight as yourself. Place the saddle on the horse, girth up and check that the centre of the seat is the lowest point. If not, the rider will be tipped backwards or forwards.

With a rider on board, the saddle should be level from front to back and the rider should be balanced, without being tipped forwards or backwards. This applies whether the saddle

has a straight or forward cut, but as explained on page 10, if the stirrup bars are positioned wrongly, the rider may find it hard to adapt a balanced seat naturally.

Stand behind the horse to see if the saddle sits evenly or is over to one side. If it is lopsided, check that the stirrup leathers are the same length and that the rider isn't putting more weight in one stirrup than the other without realizing. Also from the back, check that the saddle gullet is clear of the horse's back all the way along, including under the rider.

Check that your saddle is in the right place. A lot of riders position it too far forward; as a horse moves, the top of his shoulder blade (scapula) rotates backwards and a saddle that is wrongly placed will impede his movement. There should be a hand's width between the shoulder blade and the saddle.

The saddle on this grey horse gives sufficient clearance all the way along the back and is balanced so that the centre of the seat is the lowest point.

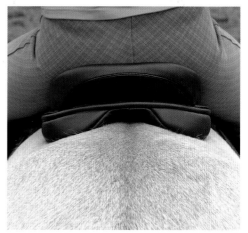

The dun pony's saddle sits evenly, allowing the rider's weight to be distributed correctly.

The pommel and cantle must clear the withers and back respectively, both when the rider is seated and when standing in the stirrups. The amount of clearance needed depends on the design of the saddle and its purpose – you usually need greater clearance for jumping than for flatwork.

The panel should give as even a bearing surface as possible – designs with a wider panel make this easier to achieve – and the saddle shouldn't bounce noticeably or swing from side to side when the horse is moving. There is bound to be some movement, because the saddle is the interface between the horse's movement and the rider trying to absorb it, but it shouldn't be excessive.

Horse and rider should be assessed in all paces, on both reins. Does the saddle look as if it sits correctly on circles and turns as well as on straight lines? If it is used for jumping, does it stay reasonably stable through all phases of the jump?

The horse's reactions can give clues to his comfort. If he shows signs of resistance, perhaps when turning in one direction or when making transitions, could the saddle be pinching or moving too much? The saddle may, of course, be nothing to do with it, but solving problems means looking at all parts of the jigsaw and saddle fit is one of them.

HIGH-TECH HELP

Sophisticated pressure analysis equipment allows fitters to see what is happening under the saddle by identifying high, medium and low-pressure areas. Not surprisingly, a combination of a balanced rider and a correctly fitted saddle scores the best readings, and an unbalanced rider can still cause problems even when riding on a well-fitting saddle.

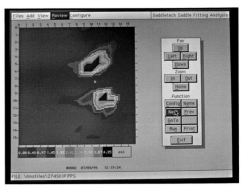

The red areas on this pressure analysis reading indicate undesirable pressure points.

A saddle with a wide panel, such as this one, helps give an even bearing surface.

TIP

Always use a mounting block when possible. Getting on from the ground puts strain on the saddle tree and can eventually twist it. It can also harm the horse's back. Many riders pull the saddle to the left when mounting, then heave it over by putting more weight in the right stirrup. Alternatively, if you and your helper are athletic enough, get a leg-up.

CONFORMATION POINTS

In some breeds and types, you'll find common conformation points that may affect saddle fit. They are not necessarily a disadvantage, but you do need to be aware of them. An experienced saddle fitter will always ask your horse or pony's breed or type when bringing a selection of saddles to fit, as this will usually help in selecting a shortlist.

Many people are now riding horses that at one time would have been used for driving or farm work, such as heavy horses and cobs with straighter shoulders (not that all cobs have straight shoulders!) This makes fitting a saddle more difficult. Obviously you don't choose a horse on the basis of how easy it will be to find a saddle that fits him, but it can be useful to keep characteristics in mind.

For instance, while cobs and some large native breeds usually have low withers and round barrels, some TBs and Warmbloods have prominent withers. Arabs, although elegant and graceful, usually need a saddle built on a wide tree.

Short-backed animals can require careful fitting, simply because there is relatively little room for a saddle. However, this is usually only significant if the rider is broad in the beam and needs a larger saddle than the horse can comfortably accommodate.

If a horse's croup is higher than his withers, he will be naturally 'downhill'. This will make him go on his forehand, and though correct schooling can compensate, your saddle may also tend to go downhill. On a horse who is herring-gutted, so that his belly 'runs up' like a greyhound or a herring, a saddle will tend to slip back.

Exceptionally high withers can make it difficult to achieve sufficient clearance under the pommel.

Arabs, such as this top endurance horse, usually need saddles built on a wide tree. This saddle is a Pegaso endurance model with a wide bearing area.

ARE YOU FITTED COMFORTABLY?

Everyone knows how important it is to fit the saddle to the horse (see page 9), but while this must take priority, the saddle must also suit and be fitted to you. If its proportions do not complement your own, you will be insecure and uncomfortable, and if it is not balanced you will struggle to achieve a balanced position. An unbalanced rider means an unbalanced horse, so take both of your needs into account.

It is important to ensure that the saddle design is suitable not just for the purpose, but for your level of riding and personal preferences. For instance, some riders like large knee rolls and others prefer to be able to adapt their position.

Make sure that the stirrup bars are sited so that they encourage a correct position: while they should be placed forward on a jumping saddle, they need to be further back on a dressage or general purpose (GP) model. Many GP saddles feature stirrup bars that naturally place your leg forward of the ideal shoulder–hip–heel vertical alignment. This leaves you either with a 'chair' seat that shifts your balance backwards, or fighting the natural forces of physics by trying to bring your legs back against the pull of the stirrups. Ask yourself whether your saddle will help you to ride well, or quite the opposite. And also ask yourself the following questions

- Does the seat size match your own? Seats are measured in 1cm (½in) increments, but other proportions alter accordingly and a rider who feels secure in a 43cm (17in) saddle may not do so in the next size up.
- Does the twist (the area from the pommel to the centre of the seat) suit your conformation and preferred discipline?
- Is the saddle balanced, so that the centre of the seat is the lowest part?
- Are the flaps the right size for your proportions?

EXPERT HELP

If riding or life in general is uncomfortable because of backache or general stiffness, consult a qualified practitioner such as a registered osteopath – someone with special knowledge of sports injuries is often ideal and can work in conjunction with your fitter to get the best results.

A good saddle fitter is your best ally in keeping you comfortable when riding, even if you have physical problems. Look for someone with wide knowledge of equine and human anatomy and a knowledge of riding who can watch you and your horse and help you choose the best options. These can range from flaps that are shorter or longer than standard to movable blocks positioned to give knee or thigh support. Your knee should not be jammed against a knee block or knee roll, but the support should be there when needed.

Many riders put more weight on one stirrup than the other, which unbalances the horse. As a temporary or, if necessary, permanent measure your expert may adjust your saddle slightly on one side to compensate. You should notice an immediate improvement, but if you later start to feel unbalanced again, call in your expert – you may have rebalanced yourself and need the saddle altered again.

'On a jumping saddle, I want a flap that allows you to get your lower leg forward in an emergency. I'm not a fan of big blocks to hold you in position – you need to be in balance with the horse and if you start to grip, with the lower leg going back, you interfere with the horse's balance and become insecure.'
Clayton Fredericks, member of the Australian eventing team

KEY

1. Seat is the correct size and puts rider in centre of saddle
2. Stirrup bars sited to allow correct leg position
3. Knee blocks positioned to allow leg to sit just behind them
4. Flaps are correct length for rider's leg proportions

BETTER BY DESIGN

Although a specialist saddle won't turn you into a superstar rider, design considerations help you achieve a balanced and therefore secure position. These include the position of the stirrup bars, the cut of the flaps and the design of the seat, so riders who enjoy more than one activity either need more than one saddle, or to compromise via a general purpose saddle.

A good GP saddle will allow you to hack, jump and school at a reasonable level. Even then, you need to decide your priorities. If flatwork comes first, a slightly straighter-cut saddle would be best; these are sometimes marketed as VSD, which originally referred to their German description but has been anglicized to Very Slightly Dressage. If you jump regularly and school your horse with jumping in mind, a more forward-cut saddle will probably be better.

But if you get serious, you need a specialist saddle suitable for the standard of your riding and your horse's way of going. For instance, some dressage saddles demand a leg position many riders are not ready for, whereas others are more suitable for those buying their first specialist design. There are key points to think about with each discipline so that you can keep your centre of gravity over the horse's.

This dressage saddle encourages a good position without being restrictive.

Dressage saddles have stirrup bars set farther back to encourage a longer, straighter leg position, but a technically correct leg position comes from overall balance. Don't buy a saddle that forces you into a position, look for one that encourages it.

Jumping saddles have stirrup bars set forward. This, combined with a shorter stirrup leather, enables the rider to close the angles of knee and thigh and keep the lower leg more forward than for flatwork when show jumping. Event riders usually shorten their stirrup leathers still further for cross-country, when jumping at speed.

Jumping saddles allow the rider – here, eventing star Mary King – to close the angles of knee and thigh.

Showing saddles set an extra challenge – they are designed to complement the horse's conformation and usually have a flatter seat and straighter flap without requiring a 'dressage position' from the rider. Those marketed as working hunter models are often the most logically designed; some showing saddles provide what is sometimes dubbed the 'lavatory seat position' because they have straight flaps with stirrup bars set relatively too far forward and flat seats.

Hot seats

Seat design is as crucial as seat size. A 'bucket' seat, sometimes described as a deep seat, may restrict you but won't actually give you a deep seat – that comes from rider ability. A flat-seated jumping saddle is preferred by many top riders because it allows them to adapt their position instantly, perhaps over a drop fence, but if you don't have their perfect balance, this style can make you feel insecure. Textured or suede seats may add security and there are even products to spray on leather to promote 'stickability' without stickiness.

Material world

If you need but are struggling to afford two saddles, or know that your or your horse's requirements will change, save money by either buying second-hand or choosing a synthetic saddle from an established manufacturer. These are smart enough for competition but half the price of leather and often have design input from professional riders and trainers.

Buying second-hand can be a minefield unless you buy from a saddler who has checked the saddle – stripping it right down if necessary and making any repairs needed – and can fit it or recommend a good fitter. Real and Internet auctions can be a huge gamble, especially if you can't inspect the saddle before buying.

Showing saddles have straighter flaps and flatter seats but don't require a 'dressage position'.

A flat-seated, particularly forward-cut saddle designed for cross-country.

This Thorowgood synthetic saddle is smart enough for competition.

'All my saddles are made from calf leather, which is hardwearing but soft. It also has a grippy quality that can be very useful at times, especially when you're going cross-country.'
Jeanette Brakewell, leading British event rider

INSIDE INFORMATION

What's inside a saddle is as important as the exterior. In most cases, it will be built on a frame called a tree, which is the equivalent of a car's chassis and gives stability and structure, though as you'll see on pages 16–17, treeless saddles have their devotees.

Modern trees are made from laminated beechwood and sprung steel, special plastics, or carbon fibre. It's generally agreed that if a tree has a degree of 'give' or flexion, the result is greater comfort for horse and rider, though different manufacturers have different ways of interpreting this: for instance, the makers of the WOW saddle (see page 17) use a patented tree that has no flexion from front to back, but has a headplate that moves from side to side to allow freedom of the shoulder blades as the horse moves.

A treed saddle can only fit a horse if the tree is the correct width and has a profile that follows the shape of the horse's back. Some trees have adjustable headplates that allow the width to be altered at the front, while the Genesis tri-form tree allows heads, seats and cantles to be changed individually within a matter of minutes.

One of the cleverest ideas is also the simplest. The Thorowgood Fish system comprises plastic inserts that slip into the saddle panels to alter the front width. However, it's still essential that the shape of the tree follows the horse's back profile.

The simple but effective Thorowgood Fish system.

BAR TALK

The tree also provides an anchoring point for the stirrup bars. As explained on page 10 (fitting saddles to riders), if these are positioned incorrectly, it's difficult or impossible to adopt a correct leg position. A few manufacturers use adjustable stirrup bars, which give much greater flexibility.

For some reason best known to the saddle industry, most bars still have a so-called safety catch designed to prevent the leathers sliding off except in an emergency. In practice, if the catch is up, it usually stays up – so always leave it in the down position.

Safety catch in the correct position.

PANEL DECISIONS

Some of the most important innovations in saddle design centre on saddle panels and what's inside them. The panel, divided by the gullet, which clears the spine, is the interface between you and your horse and should spread your weight over as wide an area as possible without causing pressure points.

Traditionally, panels are stuffed with pure wool. Many saddlers and riders still favour this; wool from the Merino sheep is said to be ideal as it is less likely to form hard lumps.

Newer alternatives include air-filled bags set inside the panels, used either alone or – perhaps a less logical option – in conjunction with flocking. The Flair airbag system has given consistently good results in pressure analysis testing and early fears from doubters that the bags would leak and/or give the sensation of riding on a beach ball proved groundless; neither durability nor rider feel are compromised.

Moulded foam panels covered with a membrane to give rapid heat exchange are another new option and are said to absorb pressure evenly once at body heat. Flexible latex panels that can be repositioned as a horse's musculature changes, or to enable the same saddle to be used on different horses, have been around for several years, but now have wider acceptance.

Seeking perfection

Everyone wants to find the best possible interface between horse and rider. There is one out there somewhere – but it might not be the same for every horse and rider, and even if maintenance is minimal, most riders still need a saddle-fitting specialist to set up and periodically adjust a system.

Opinions vary on what works best, and the only answer is to weigh up the arguments, try different systems and see how your horse reacts. Good retailers and fitters should be able to arrange some sort of trial, which may involve a short rental period.

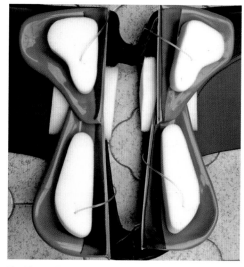

The Flair airbag system gives consistently good pressure testing results.

Traditionally, panels are stuffed with pure wool.

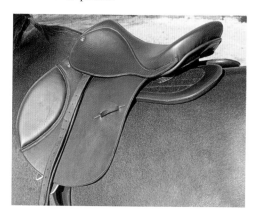

The ReacorPanel saddle has movable, flexible panels.

GOING TREELESS

Going treeless is an option that is becoming increasingly popular. As with treed saddles, there are wide differences in standards of design and manufacture, and you must not assume that one particular saddle will suit all horses and all riders.

The advantage of treeless saddles is that they allow more flexibility in fitting, especially when the design allows customization with, perhaps, different shims or pads. It's also clear that some horses go better in a treeless saddle that suits them and the rider, though this may be because their previous treed saddles were an unsatisfactory fit.

Initial tests by the UK Society of Master Saddlers, using the Pliance pressure mapping system, have led it to state that it has not found any advantage in using a treeless saddle over a well-fitting treed saddle. It found high, localized pressure under the stirrup bars on all the treeless models it tested, though these have not been identified and the readings improved when single-thickness stirrup leathers were used.

Possible disadvantages are that some have an unconventional appearance and may also offer less comfort and security for the rider. This is usually because there is no defined waist or twist, so the seat is uncomfortably wide. Also, some saddles have good side-to-side stability, but may tend to slip forwards, especially when riding downhill.

If you're not concerned about conventional appearance, there are plenty of designs to consider. However, if you are, the most acceptable saddle will probably be

one of the Fhoenix flexible concept range, designed by trainer Heather Moffett, founder of Enlightened Equitation. Manufactured in the UK, it is now available worldwide.

Strictly speaking, it isn't treeless, as there is a small, rigid cantle – but as it can't be felt by horse or rider, this is splitting hairs. It has either a Prolite panel or a detachable Suberpanel; the latter is filled with cork granules that mould to the horse's shape.

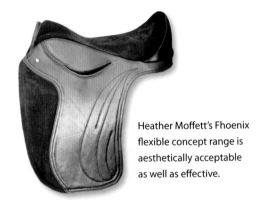

Heather Moffett's Fhoenix flexible concept range is aesthetically acceptable as well as effective.

'Having no points of a tree means that the [horse's] shoulders are much less restricted, while lateral flexibility means that the saddle will allow the horse's back to round up and carry the rider more easily, also allowing the rider to feel the movement of the horse in a way that I believe treed saddles don't permit.'
Heather Moffett, international trainer and founder of Enlightened Equitation

LASTING BENEFITS?

Some manufacturers argue that while a good-quality, conventional treed saddle will last for 15 or more years, treeless saddles have a much shorter life and so are relatively more expensive. By definition, modern designs haven't been around long enough to prove their durability, but for some riders, they are becoming not just the first choice but the only choice.

Making adjustments

While lots of saddles allow you to make minor adjustments through movable knee and thigh blocks and adjustable gullets, the WOW saddle goes even farther. Designed by engineer David Kempsell, who developed the Flair air flocking system, it is built on a carbon-fibre tree without conventional points, thus removing a common pressure-point area.

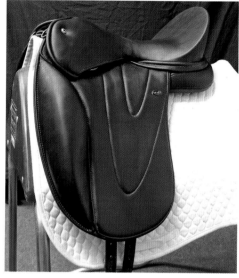

The WOW saddle has interchangeable seats, flaps and panels.

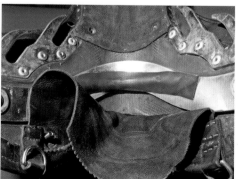

The WOW saddle tree allows freedom of the horse's shoulder blades.

It also has interchangeable seats, flaps and panels as well as clever design points. A deliberate 'step' between the seat and flap gives a slight hollow, allowing the inner thigh muscle to fall into place, and the flaps can be moved to suit different leg lengths.

The seat can also be customized to alleviate the discomfort a lot of riders – women in particular – suffer but feel embarrassed to admit. The skirts over the stirrup bars can be padded to give more support in front of the thigh, thus raising the rider's fork off the front of the saddle.

All seat models are fitted with a double stirrup bar, giving a choice of two leg positions. This allows fine-tuning on specialist dressage and jumping saddles and, on GP and VSD models, means that you can more easily adopt the correct leg positions for flatwork and jumping instead of simply altering the length of your stirrup leathers.

WESTERN SADDLES

Western-style riding is often misunderstood by English-style riders, who tend to think of it as 'playing cowboys'. Instead, it offers a range of disciplines – including reining, which is likely to achieve Olympic status by 2012 – and a wide range of saddles has been developed to suit the different demands.

Construction is basically similar to that of English-style saddles, but with differences in terminology; for instance, a girth is a cinch and instead of stirrup leathers there are wide fenders designed to protect the rider's legs. Many, but not all, Western saddles are 'double-rigged' with two cinches for stability.

Parade (show) and some pleasure saddles can be highly decorated, with silver inlay and embossed leather. Saddles designed for tougher jobs are usually plainer and there are subtle differences between specialist models.

The stock saddle is the closest to the English-style GP and gives great rider security. It is often a secret weapon in the tack rooms of those who take on wayward horses, as it can help the rider survive bucks and spins.

Trail and pleasure saddles are the next step up in refinement, with a high cantle and more pronounced curve to the seat.

Roping saddles have substantial horns for anchoring the roped calf or steer, front and flank cinches for stability and a low front and cantle to both allow the rider freedom of

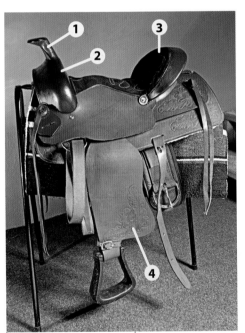

This highly decorated Mexican saddle, complete with lariat and knife, is a real talking point – the horn is covered with skin from a bull's scrotum!

KEY

1 Horn	3 Cantle
2 Swell	4 Fender

movement and reduce pressure on the horse's withers. Cutting saddles have high swells and horns, which can act as a grab handle or leverage point when cutting a calf from the herd; a good cutting horse will read the situation as well as or better than his rider, and the hardest part of the rider's job is often to stay with him.

Barrel racing is the speed discipline, and the saddles used have a deep seat for rider stability, often textured for grip. A high swell gives stability and the horn is designed to allow the rider to hold on round sharp turns.

Reining, sometimes dubbed Western dressage, demands feel and sensitivity. Accordingly, reining saddles have seats that allow the rider to tilt the pelvis back for sliding stops and a low horn that doesn't interfere with the reins or the rider's hands.

Decorative silver inlays are a feature of Western saddles used for parade or show purposes.

FITTING FACTS

There is a misconception among some riders that as long as the seat accommodates the rider, any Western saddle will fit any horse. In fact, it's just as important that a knowledgeable specialist selects and fits a saddle with a correct tree and swell for individual combinations.

Trees can be made from rawhide-covered wood, which combines strength with a little give and is stronger and longer lasting than plastic or wood covered with canvas or other material. The bars – the part that rests along the horse's back – are of different sizes, shapes and angles to accommodate different back shapes.

The angle of the bars, together with the design of the swell, affects the shape and height of the gullet. A knowledgeable fitter can choose the right combination to ensure the saddle clears the spine and withers and spreads the rider's weight evenly.

Adult seat sizes range from 35.5 to 45.5cm (14 to 18in) and are measured from the centre back of the swell to the centre of the cantle. English saddles are measured from the front stud diagonally across to the centre of the cantle.

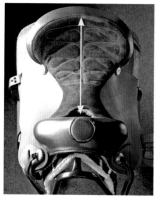
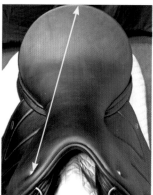

Western and English saddle seats are measured in different ways. Note the pronounced curve to the seat of the trail saddle (left).

GOING SIDEWAYS

Riding side-saddle, English- or Western-style, is enjoying a worldwide popularity boom – you can show, compete in show jumping or dressage, hunt, team chase or ride for pleasure. Good side saddles are often harder to find and harder to fit than astride models, so specialist help is vital.

Many riders rely on finding side saddles made in the 1900s by classic makers such as Owen, Mayhew and Champion and Wilton, as fewer modern saddlers are able to make them. This is not just because of the specialist skills, but because there are currently only two companies manufacturing side-saddle trees in the UK and none in the USA.

Even wide cobs can be side-saddle stars, as leading English show rider Lynn Russell proves.

FITTING CHALLENGE

The big problem with saddles from the 1900s is that they were designed for narrow Thoroughbred types with defined withers. Today, the emphasis is on wider horses who carry more weight – both their own and that of their rider.

Stability can also be a problem, especially if the horse doesn't have a defined wither – though the combination of a balanced rider and an expert fitter can ensure that even wide cobs and natives can be side-saddle stars. Much can be achieved through flocking and many fitters advocate a pad called a Wykeham pad, which allows flexibility in fitting different back conformations. This is a thick felt pad used under a side saddle that has a tree but no panels, and is especially suitable for wider horses.

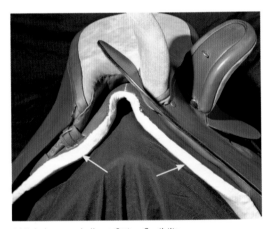

A Wykeham pad allows fitting flexibility.

Proportions must also suit the rider and most vintage saddles used today would originally have been made to measure for their first lady owner. Seats are flat and if too narrow for the rider's seat can cause discomfort. It's also important that the size and position of the fixed head (upper pommel) and leaping head (lower pommel) complement the length of the rider's leg from the back of the knee to the hip.

Side saddles are usually secured with a girth, an overgirth and a balance strap. The balance strap is designed to keep the weight of the saddle even on the horse's back.

Western ways

In the USA, side-saddle Western-style has a big following, both for pleasure and for show. The first true Western side saddle is said to be the Goodnight saddle, developed in 1892 by Colonel Charles Goodnight, who had it made so that his wife, Maryann, could ride effectively and safely on cattle drives. The modern Western-style side saddle has a dipped rather than a flat seat and is usually decorated rather than plain.

Treeless or not?

Although treeless astride saddles are finding favour, this isn't yet a feasible option for side saddles for adult riders. This style of riding demands a saddle that remains stable and expert makers say that a treeless saddle combined with an adult's weight would produce too much movement.

However, Pilch saddles, which have a front arch but no tree, are sometimes used for children starting their side-saddle careers.

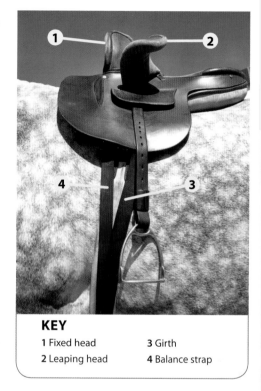

KEY

1 Fixed head   3 Girth
2 Leaping head 4 Balance strap

Go slow

Don't assume that because a horse is well schooled astride, he will automatically accept a side saddle. Most do, but it needs to be introduced carefully. Some resent the balance strap at first, so adjust it fairly loosely at first and lead him on both reins until he accepts it. Tighten it gradually until he is relaxed and the saddle is secure for mounting.

Side saddles are heavy and most experts advise that they should not be used until a horse is six or seven years old and his back is fully developed.

'The whole idea of the English-style side saddle is that the rider sits on a platform and remains still and elegant. They are flocked up firmer than English saddles and the whole construction is rigid.

Western saddles are usually made for the wider type of horse, such as the Quarter Horse. They are more forgiving to the rider because they hold her in place so securely – horses tend to go nicely because the rider is kept stable and so doesn't interfere with the horse's balance.'

Laura Dempsey, side-saddle maker and fitter in the UK and USA

UNDER THE SADDLE

Saddle pads, numnahs and cloths range from simple designs to absorb sweat and keep the saddle clean to high-tech products. Some are said to aid shock absorption or stability whereas others are designed to alter the saddle balance or fit. Numnahs aren't always essential – some people believe that a leather or serge saddle lining is the best interface between the saddle and the horse's back – but can often be valuable.

PADDING PITFALLS

In some cases, using anything other than a thin numnah under a well-fitting saddle can cause problems – instead of giving a cushioning effect, it can be the equivalent of wearing three pairs of socks in a pair of shoes that fitted well with just one.

Make sure that whatever you use, it's pulled up into the saddle gullet so as not to put pressure over the withers. The best designs are cut and shaped to help with this.

Check too that securing straps are positioned to suit your saddle, as otherwise the numnah will be pulled down. If necessary, get them removed and repositioned. You also need to make sure that the numnah is big enough to fit under your saddle without the edging getting caught, as this in itself could cause rubs and pressure points.

Pads and numnahs should be adjusted so as not to put pressure on the withers.

MATERIAL WORLD

Some fabrics offer special benefits. Pure wool allows air circulation and some pressure testing has shown that it helps minimize pressure points. It can be left on the sheepskin or woven on to a cloth back; the latter is easier to wash.

Pure wool felt pads are popular in the USA and 'breathe' well, but because they are quite thick, may alter the fit of a saddle. Leather pads were used in the Spanish Riding School of Vienna and are recommended by some American saddle-fitting experts; the stiffness of the leather is said to help prevent pressure points reaching the horse's back.

Gel pads were hailed as the answer when they first appeared. However, pressure analysis has shown that in some cases improvement is temporary and because gel moves, pressure may be relieved from one spot but form in another.

If saddle stability is a problem, which often happens with horses and ponies who have round barrels and undefined withers, there are ideas to help. These range from numnahs incorporating 'grippy' materials to thin, shaped pads made from trademarked materials such as Prolite.

The Barnsby grip pad has panels which help the saddle stay in place.

TIP

Showing riders traditionally do not use numnahs or pads, believing that these detract from appearance. But if your horse needs one, some companies will make to measure from a template of your saddle. Some astride and side-saddle riders use a chamois leather, cut to fit, underneath their saddles to minimize slipping.

A brown sheepskin numnah made from a template of this showing saddle.

FIT AND BALANCE

While pads can be used to alter the balance and fit of the saddle temporarily, nothing can turn a badly fitting saddle into one that fits well. However, there are approaches that many riders find successful.

Using pads of different shapes and thicknesses is an integral part of the system advocated by Balance International – an organization based in the UK but which works regularly in the USA and Canada. Its founders advocate using saddles that are wider than a horse's current static profile together with a system of pads to encourage correct muscle build-up.

Shims, thin pads that can be used to alter the balance of the saddle at the front or back, are often used as a temporary measure to adjust saddle balance. On yards where there is a rapidly changing horse population and it is impossible to have a saddle for each horse, they may be standard equipment, but it takes a knowledgeable eye to use them successfully.

Other ideas have included pads filled with cork granules or polystyrene beads, said to provide an interface that moulds to the horse's shape in use. However, nothing can solve the problem of a saddle that is too narrow.

One of the most successful and flexible products is the Korrector, from the same manufacturers as the Flair airbag system. It too uses four airbags, this time inserted in a pocketed saddle cloth.

The manufacturers stress that this design will work with saddles that fit correctly and with those that are too wide – but not with those that are too narrow.

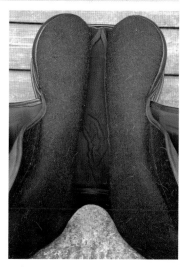

Although most modern saddles have leather panels, some manufacturers are going back to traditional serge. It is said to be warmer and, when the saddle is correctly flocked, give good results on pressure testing analysis. Serge should be brushed and allowed to dry and most riders like to use a thin cotton numnah to prevent hairs sticking to it.

GIRTHS

The type of girth you use and the way you adjust it depends on many factors. One of the most important – which is often forgotten – is the horse's conformation.

All horses have a natural girth line, where the belly starts to curve upwards just behind the forelegs, and the girth settles naturally. The ideal girth line is about 10cm (4in) behind the elbow, but in many horses it is farther forward or back. This, coupled with the shape of the horse's shoulder, makes it harder to prevent a saddle slipping forwards or back.

If the girth groove is too close to the elbow, the saddle will tend to move forwards – and if the horse's scapula is not well defined, this makes things worse. If the girth line is further back than is ideal, the saddle will tend to slip back and if this is coupled with a pronounced scapula and/or a straight back, the problem will be more pronounced.

However, there are strategies to help – see the Q and A section on pages 28–9.

All horses have a natural girth line (arrowed).

'As water finds its own level, a girth will settle in the narrowest part of the horse's barrel.'
The late Barry Richardson, master saddler and inventor of the ReactorPanel saddle

GIVE AND TAKE

Girths are made from many different types of material, including leather, webbing, neoprene and cord. The best incorporate equal 'give' throughout their length; this also helps to prevent them being over tightened.

Research from Australia shows that when girths are fastened too tightly, the horse's stride length may be restricted. Obviously, it also causes discomfort.

Shaping can also make a girth more or less comfortable. If it is shaped away from the elbow, it is less likely to pinch and if it is relatively broad across the centre line of the underbelly, it will be more comfortable and more stable. Girths with built-in studguards (see Q and A section, pages 28–9) often have the added benefit of spreading pressure over a wider area.

This girth is shaped to provide security and minimize the risk of pinching.

An Albion girth with elastic inserts at both ends, far preferable to designs with an insert at one end.

Studguards provide protection and also spread pressure over a wider area.

This girth incorporates stretch throughout its length.

TIP

Many girths have elastic inserts at one or both ends. Those with inserts at one end only are not recommended, as it is impossible to get tension balanced throughout the girth. They may also contribute to the saddle slipping to one side.

If you do have to use a girth of this type, adjust it from the side without inserts so you do not inadvertently fasten it too tightly.

The right lengths

Traditionally, dressage girths are shorter than those for other disciplines, to minimize bulk under the rider's legs. Girth straps on dressage saddles are therefore correspondingly longer.

Make sure the girth is long enough, though; many riders use dressage girths that are too short and the buckles knock the horse's elbows as he moves. Some manufacturers are now making GP saddles to take dressage girths, as they believe that the principle of the less bulk the better applies more widely.

Girths should be fastened on the same holes on each side to aid stability, with enough leeway for adjustment. This can be difficult when elastic inserts are fitted on one end only – another good reason for not using this design.

Don't rush the girthing process, even if you're in a hurry. Fasten it just tightly enough to keep the saddle in place, then tighten gradually until you can fit only the flat of your hand between the girth and the horse's belly.

This should give enough security – though you'll need to check when you're mounted and again a few minutes later, as some horses always blow themselves out to start with. *Always* stretch the horse's legs forward before mounting, to avoid skin being pinched.

STIRRUPS AND LEATHERS

Stirrups and leathers might sound to be rather boring basics, but new ideas and materials have a lot to offer. Whatever your interest, they must be chosen with your safety and comfort in mind.

The strongest stirrup leathers were traditionally those made from buffalo hide – which remain a favourite with polo players – oxhide and rawhide. Their big disadvantage is that they stretch – and as most of us put more weight in one stirrup than the other, it's essential to swap them from side to side each time you ride.

Modern alternatives include leather wrapped round a nylon core, which gives strength and smartness without stretching. Synthetic leathers are strong and these too don't stretch, but can cause rub marks on leather saddles. However, they are the ideal choice for synthetic saddles; it's best to use ones made by your saddle's manufacturer, as materials will have been chosen to complement each other.

Designs that adjust near the stirrup iron rather than the bar minimize bulk under the leg and are popular for dressage, but can't be adjusted easily, and therefore safely, when you are mounted.

ANY OLD IRONS?

Most stirrups for English-style riding are made from stainless steel for safety and durability. Brass and brass alloys are also popular, especially in the USA, and aluminium is used to make lightweight irons for racing.

Standard stirrups have been joined by many new designs, but whether you ride for pleasure or in competition, the most important considerations are safety and suitability. To minimize the risk of your foot being trapped in a fall, make sure stirrups are the right size, and consider using one of the special safety designs.

The general rule is that stirrups should be 19mm– 2.5cm (¾–1in) wider than the widest part of your boot. Check that those used with leather competition boots allow enough room for heavier everyday or winter ones – or if necessary, use different stirrups.

Safety first
Traditional Peacock safety stirrups with rubber rings on the outside should *only* be used by lightweight children. The weight of the average teenager or adult stresses even stainless steel and may cause it to break, as the tread is supported only on one side.

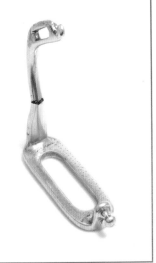

This stainless steel Peacock safety iron broke when used by an adult rider – the design is only suitable for small children.

Special safety designs range from the Australian Simplex or bent leg design to those with hinged sides that release in a fall. The Mountain Horse SC3 stirrup system goes even further and combines a range of riding boots with soles designed to interface with the treads in the range's safety stirrups, which have quick-release sides.

The Mountain Horse SC3 stirrup system comprises boots and stirrups with interfacing surfaces.

The Australian Simplex or bent leg iron.

COMFORT AND POSITION

Modern designs with hinged or multi-jointed sides are said to reduce stress on the rider's joints and to help achieve a correct leg position with the heel slightly down. Other ideas for encouraging a correct leg position include angled rubber stirrup treads and irons with offset eyes.

Most English stirrups have relatively narrow treads, which put pressure on a smaller area of the foot. Endurance and Western riders use stirrups with wider treads, which are more comfortable when riding for long periods; some riders also prefer these for pleasure riding and schooling.

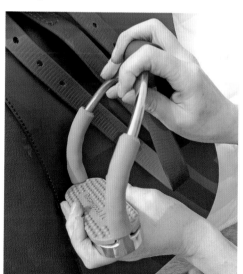

Another idea for safety and comfort – the multi-jointed Thorowgood T6 stirrup.

Endurance and Western stirrups have a broader tread.

QUESTIONS AND ANSWERS

Q My partner and I are buying a 15.1hh (155cm) lightweight show cob that will be suitable for both of us – I'm 1.6m (5ft 4in) and 57kg (9 stone) and my partner is 1.8m (6ft) and weighs 83kg (13 stone). I will be the main rider, but how do we choose a saddle that will suit the horse, be comfortable for each of us and that I can use in the show ring?

A It's always difficult to suit two riders who have very different builds, but there are strategies that can help. The horse's comfort must take top priority and if one partner will be riding much more frequently than the other, he or she comes next in line.

As you intend to show your cob, you must also ensure that your saddle is comfortable for ride judges, many of whom will be larger than you. The best solution may be to use a saddle that is slightly larger in the seat than you need, but not so large that you feel insecure: while you would probably be comfortable in a 43cm (17in) saddle, a 44.5cm (17½in) would be better for larger riders.

You may also need to buy an extra set of stirrups and leathers for your partner – and judges – who will very probably have larger feet than you. When you go in the ring, get your helper to bring them in before the judge rides your horse and swap them over.

The other solution is to buy a leather saddle to suit your needs and a cheaper second-hand leather or new synthetic one for your partner.

Q I need to make a template of the area behind my horse's withers so that my saddler knows which of the saddles she has in stock are likely to fit. What's the easiest way to do this?

A The simplest and cheapest way is to use a Flexicurve, a flexible strip used by designers and architects for drawing curves, available from most art shops. Find the point of the horse's scapula and take your measurement a hand's width behind it, moulding the Flexicurve over the horse. Press it gently in so it is in contact on both sides; then remove it, place it on a sheet of paper and trace along the inside edge.

Use a Flexicurve to measure your horse's wither profile.

The Equiform is a more sophisticated method and gives a 3D picture of the horse's back. It is made from special plastic that is heated in water, cooled and moulded over the horse.

Q Despite professional fitting, my New Forest pony's saddle tends to slip forwards, possibly because he has very low withers and a slightly straight shoulder. Is there anything I can do?

A Try using the front two girth straps instead of the usual first and third ones, combined with a numnah or saddle cloth designed to aid stability.

Q I broke my pelvis some years ago and however hard I try, I put more weight in the right stirrup than the left. This makes my saddle sit slightly to the right and I'm worried that this will make my horse uncomfortable. Is there anything I can do?

A Find a good osteopath or other registered practitioner who can make sure you're as comfortable and balanced as possible. You also need a good saddle fitter who can watch you and your horse in action and adjust your saddle to compensate for your imbalance by raising the saddle under your right seatbone.

Although this can be done with a wool-flocked saddle, it's usually easier to fine-tune adjustments when a saddle is fitted with the Flair system – though this obviously depends on the skill of the fitter, too.

Q How do you solve the opposite problem – the saddle that slips back?

A In this case, using the two rear girth straps, again combined with a 'grippy' numnah or saddle cloth, might solve the problem. If this isn't enough, your saddler may suggest positioning the rear girth strap further back.

A breastplate or breastgirth (see pages 88–9) may give you extra security.

Q I have arthritis in my hips and, unfortunately, my cob has a bouncy stride. My saddle is comfortable and fits both of us, but I still get discomfort on a long ride. Is there anything that can help?

A Try a combination of stirrup irons with hinged or flexible sides, which will help you absorb your horse's movement through your ankles, knees and hips, and a good seat saver. The one shown here is designed by Heather Moffett and incorporates special foam used in pilots' ejector seats.

2 CONTENTS

BITS

BITTING ISSUES

Bitting often causes more confusion and controversy than any other area of tack and equipment. But although it's a complex subject, it can be broken down into simple objectives.

Whichever bit you choose, there are three vital considerations: your horse's mouth and teeth must be in good condition, the mouthpiece should suit the conformation of your horse's mouth, and the bit must be the correct size and adjusted properly.

OPEN WIDE

Regular dental checks by a good equine vet or qualified dental technician will ensure your horse is comfortable, and any sharp edges on the cheek teeth can be rasped (floated). Routine annual checks are enough for some horses, but others need six-monthly ones.

If you get any problems in between – such as quidding, where your horse drops food as he eats, or resistances such as head tossing or setting the jaw – get him checked immediately. You can help make sure his teeth meet and wear evenly by feeding him from the ground, mimicking the natural grinding pattern of grazing.

Talk to your vet or technician about the latest ideas and how they relate to your horse. For instance, at one time the removal of shallow-rooted wolf teeth was standard practice, but many experts now prefer to follow the philosophy of 'If it ain't broke, don't fix it' and leave them unless they definitely cause problems by coming into contact with the bit.

Bit seats, said to help the bit lie more comfortably and made by rounding the first cheek teeth, became very fashionable but are now less so. However, every case is individual.

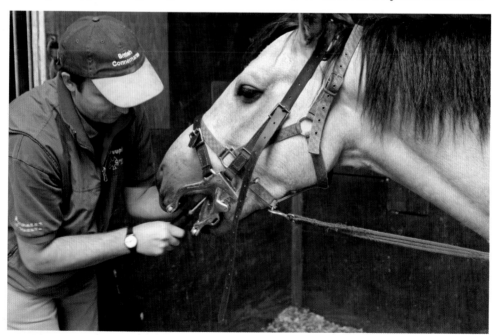

MOUTH CONFORMATION

Many riders never think about the shape of their horse's mouth, but it's a key factor when choosing or changing bits.

Start on the outside and look at whether your horse has fleshy lips that wrinkle easily. Also, is he short from the end of his muzzle to the corner of his lips? Both are factors you must take into consideration when adjusting the height of his bit.

Get someone to hold your horse on a headcollar and part his lips gently. Does his tongue bulge out at the sides of his teeth? If so, this affects the thickness of bit and type of mouthpiece he will be comfortable with. Now slide a finger gently into his mouth and rest it on the bars, where the bit lies. Crook your finger slightly to assess how much of a gap there is, if any, between the bars and the roof of his mouth, as this will also affect which type of mouthpiece he will find comfortable.

Check for rubs or pinches on the corners of his mouth and inside his lip. If you find these or other problems, such as ulcers, wait until they are healed and get veterinary advice if necessary. Then use the advice on the following pages, plus your new knowledge of his mouth conformation, to find a suitable bit.

IN GOOD HANDS

Any bit can only be as good as the person using it. This book will help you choose the right one for your horse's mouth conformation, and even help you solve problems, but you should always consider that your riding may be the root cause of any difficulties.

And what seems to be a mouth problem may be a case of a horse demonstrating problems that lie elsewhere. It may even be that he is being asked to do something he finds too difficult and is demonstrating this by mouth resistances.

DIMENSIONS AND CONDITION

The length of a bit mouthpiece is measured as shown below and its thickness is taken as the diameter of the widest part, near the rings or cheeks. A thick bit has a wider bearing surface, so is theoretically milder than a thinner one – but some horses don't have room in their mouths for thick bits and are more comfortable with thinner ones.

Check your horse's mouth for rubs and pinches.

Curb and pelham cheeks (shanks) are usually measured from top to bottom, and standard proportions are that the shank will be the same length as the mouthpiece. However, if you want more or less leverage, look for bits with cheeks that are correspondingly longer or shorter.

Check bits regularly for signs of wear, and remember that really cheap bits are often cheap because they are of inferior quality. In particular, watch out for sharp areas round the holes of loose ring snaffles, and bits that could pinch through wear or inferior manufacture. For instance, many horses go well in snaffles with alternate stainless steel and copper rollers, but because copper is softer, it wears more quickly, leading to rubbing or pinching. Be aware of this risk when using any bit incorporating different types of metal.

Some materials can be damaged by horses' teeth even when the latter are in good condition.

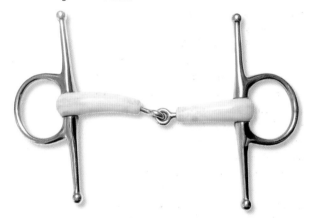

TIP

Rubber, plastics and other materials can't withstand horses' teeth, even when bits are well made and of good quality. Cheap copies of well-known designs are often even quicker to distort, as shown above.

A thick bit is theoretically milder, but some horses' mouths can't accommodate them and they will be happier with a thinner mouthpiece.

FITTING GUIDELINES

To fit comfortably, bits must have a correctly sized mouthpiece and be adjusted at the optimum height. As always, there are rules, and exceptions to them. Start with the guidelines below and adapt as necessary.

The mouthpiece must be long enough to prevent cheekpieces rubbing or pinching, but not so wide that it slides from side to side. Many people use bits that are too long: this means that even when the bit appears to be at the right height in the mouth, single or double joints hang too low and, because there is too much sideways movement, can be pulled off-centre.

As a guideline, when a loose ring-jointed bit is straightened in the horse's mouth, there should be no more than 1cm (½in) between the hole on each side and the horse's lips. A bit with fixed cheeks, such as an eggbutt or D-ring, can

fit slightly more snugly, but the cheeks must not pinch or rub. Remember that a bit should remain central in the horse's mouth for clear communication and comfort.

Waterford bits, which have multi-jointed mouthpieces and are available as snaffles and pelhams, are the exception. Because they wrap round the horse's lower jaw, they should protrude slightly more on each side to avoid pinching: see page 39.

Fitting a double bridle correctly means, of course, that you are fitting two bits at the same time. See pages 52–3 for information.

SIZE ISSUES

Some bit manufacturers use imperial measurements and some metric. It is helpful to have both options when trying to fit the horse who is between sizes, as so often happens. (It is possible to have bits made to measure, but also very expensive.) You may also find bits that measure slightly larger or smaller than the stated size, so never buy a bit without measuring it.

If you own a young horse, as he grows, you may find that his mouth gets bigger, too. Don't assume that the bit that fits him perfectly as a just-backed three-year-old will still be the correct size when he reaches physical maturity; some breeds and types grow until they are about seven years old.

Assessing your horse's mouth conformation will help you assess the correct height of his bit – look at him as an individual rather than aiming to see a certain number of wrinkles at the side of the mouth. If he has fleshy lips, there will be more wrinkles.

The bit in this horse's mouth is too large – this will slide through and bang against the sides of the mouth. It will also hang too low in the mouth.

The bit should be at a comfortable height, and not pull the horse's mouth into a false grin.

The bit should lie comfortably across the bars of the mouth, so that it neither pulls the mouth into a false grin nor hangs so low that the horse puts his tongue over it. A tiny adjustment can sometimes make a huge difference: this can be as little as raising or lowering the bit by one hole on one side, then carefully repositioning the bridle so the bit is centred in the mouth.

The multi-jointed Waterford snaffle should be slightly wider than other designs to avoid pinching.

Check whether a bit needs to go a particular way round in the horse's mouth. The makers of the KK Ultra, a popular lozenge snaffle, have eliminated the risk of mistakes – all you have to do is make sure that the arrow faces forward when the bit is in place.

'If your horse tends to carry his head too high for his stage of training, lowering the bit by a hole can encourage him to lower his head. If he carries it too low, raise it slightly.'
Jennie Loriston-Clarke, international dressage trainer and rider

FAMILIES, FACTS AND FALLACIES

There are thousands of different bits, which are traditionally grouped into four families – snaffles, pelhams and kimblewicks, double bridles and gag bits – together with an important extra group, bitless bridles. Modern riders need to add an extra family: combination bits incorporating nosebands. Combination designs go back many years, but systems such as those by Myler and Mikmar (see pages 54–55) are hugely popular.

Some horses are so well made they are 'born on the bit.'

Bits and bridles can act on several control points and their action may change according to the horse's head carriage – which, in turn, varies according to the level of training and to conformation. Some horses are so well made they are 'born on the bit', whereas others struggle to make the most of what nature gave them.

For instance, when a horse is at the beginning of his training, or isn't schooled, his head carriage is fairly low and his nose in front of

When a horse works in an educated outline, his face is on the vertical.

The Danger bit.

The Wilkie snaffle.

the vertical. This means a snaffle will have an upward action.

As he starts to come off his forehand, and his nose is only slightly in front of the vertical, the bit will act more on the lower jaw – and when he works in an educated outline with his face on the vertical, it will focus contact on the lower jaw without any 'lifting' action.

Adding a particular design of noseband, martingale or training aid may also affect a bit's action. For instance, using a drop noseband with a snaffle increases the emphasis of the bit's contact on the bars of the mouth and often encourages a horse to drop his head slightly.

Similarly, a running martingale helps to keep the rein contact stable, which can make a horse ridden by beginners, or by more experienced riders with unsteady hands, more comfortable.

WHAT'S IN A NAME?

Bits are sometimes given confusing names and some are known by more than one. For instance, the three-ring snaffle is also known as a Continental snaffle, a bubble snaffle, a Pessoa and even a fat lady bit. It's also referred to as a Dutch or three-ring gag, but doesn't really fit into that category (see page 45).

Similarly, while some show-pony producers are happy for children to ride in a so-called Globe pelham, which is actually a short-cheeked curb, others have criticized beval bits such as the Wilkie snaffle, believing that it has a gag action, which is untrue.

The cleverest and cheekiest name of any bit must be that thought of by some manufacturers of the Cambridge mouth snaffle, which has the same mouthpiece as the kimblewick on page 47, but with loose rings and no curb chain. It's sometimes marketed as the Magic bit, something we'd all love to find but which will never exist.

> **What's in a name?**
> One of the most curious names is that given to the Danger bit range. No one seems to have any idea of why it has been marketed as this – suggestions on a postcard, please?

'I've had a lot of success with snaffles in the Danger range. They have a central lozenge and the sides of the mouthpiece bend to a certain point, then stop, so the mouthpiece changes almost to a mullen one.'
Di Fisher, UK Grand Prix dressage rider and trainer

The three-ring snaffle has a variety of names and is available with a variety of mouthpieces – this one has a French link.

The cleverly named Magic bit – if only there was such a thing!

MOUTHPIECES

Mouthpieces can be straight, curved, or have one or more joints. They can have central lozenges, arches (ports) plates or rollers and can even be designed and marketed as part of a bitting system, as with Myler bits (see page 54). So what's the difference?

Straight bar bits don't allow room for the tongue, so mullen (slightly arched) ones are nearly always a better choice. Some people accept mullen mouth pelhams happily but have an irrational dislike of mullen mouth snaffles, claiming they are not subtle enough.

In fact, they give clear signals and many horses like them. They often suit horses and ponies with short mouths and/or low palates, because they can be adjusted at the correct height without pulling up the lips too far.

Straight or curved plastic- or rubber-covered mouthpieces often have some flexibility. This allows them to follow the shape of the horse's mouth, often a comfort factor.

Ported mouthpieces, found on snaffles such as the Myler snaffle below, pelhams, kimblewicks and curbs, allow extra room for the tongue. It used to be thought that this meant that the mouthpiece acted directly on the bars, without the tongue being able to act as a cushion, but X-rays have in fact proved otherwise.

Traditional single-jointed bits have a squeezing action and the straighter the arms, the sharper the squeeze.

Check that single-jointed bits are made correctly. One arm should be slightly longer than the other so that when rein contact is taken up and the bit arms fold, the joint remains central and the rider doesn't inadvertently put more pressure on one side than the other.

Double-jointed mouthpieces include those with French links, lozenges and Dr Bristol mouthpieces. All lie in a curve rather than in the V-shape of the single-jointed bit and many horses prefer them.

All these mouthpieces reduce the amount of tongue pressure, except the Dr Bristol, which applies it. It's therefore vital not to confuse the latter with the similar-looking French link. The French link, described much more accurately in the USA as the dogbone, has curved sides whereas the Dr Bristol's central link is flat-sided.

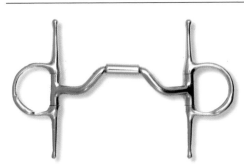

A Myler snaffle with a ported mouthpiece.

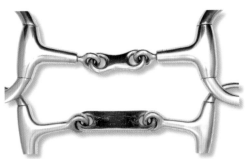

Don't confuse the French link mouthpiece, where the central section has curved sides and tongue pressure is reduced, with the flat-sided Dr Bristol, which applies tongue pressure.

Tongue pressure doesn't have to be bad. If a strong horse or pony becomes lighter in the hand when ridden in a Dr Bristol, thus avoiding a tug of war, both rider and horse will be more comfortable. The French link mouthpiece is permitted under FEI dressage rules, but the Dr Bristol cannot be used in this discipline.

The multi-jointed Waterford mouthpiece, usually seen on snaffles but also available with pelham cheeks, is one of the most underrated. Often described as severe, it's actually one that many horses accept straight away, as long as the rider has good hands, because it follows the shape of the mouth and also encourages the horse to salivate.

Rollers can be set within the mouthpiece, as in a Magenis snaffle, or round it, as with a cherry roller snaffle. Their constant movement often encourages the horse to mouth the bit and may discourage him from trying to grab or lean on it, but because roller mouthpieces are invariably single jointed with straight arms, they have a marked squeezing action.

Cherry roller and Magenis snaffles.

Twisted mouthpieces are not, as some riders believe, always severe, but they always have this potential. A snaffle with a loose (slow) twist in good hands, used as a 'refresher', can help lighten a horse who leans by acting on different parts of the tongue and mouth. A tight (fast) twist has a sharper action.

Some bits have reversible mouthpieces, smooth on one side and twisted or ridged on the other.

The Waterford snaffle follows the shape of the mouth.

A loose or slow twist snaffle.

MATERIAL WORLD

The material from which a mouthpiece is made can have a huge influence on its acceptability to the horse. They literally have different tastes, so while there are general guidelines, there will always be a horse who confounds expectations.

Stainless steel is relatively cheap and doesn't bend. The fact that it doesn't rust used to be considered an asset, but ideas have come full circle and oxidization – marketing-speak for rusting – is often recommended as a way of promoting salivation.

Sweet iron bits gradually rust, without harming the horse, and are popular in English and Western riding. The old horse breakers and nagsmen deliberately used rusty bits to encourage youngsters to accept them, and sweet iron is the modern rider's acceptable alternative.

WET, WET, WET

So why encourage a horse to salivate? If he has a dry mouth, a bit will cause friction, particularly over the bars. This leads to discomfort and possible injury. However, a wet mouth allows the bit to glide over the bars.

Don't confuse a horse who mouths the bit and relaxes his jaw with one who chews and chomps because he is tense or uncomfortable. And don't forget that if you strap his mouth shut, he won't be able to relax his jaw (see nosebands, pages 64–5).

Copper also encourages salivation, but doesn't wear well alone (see the example of the D-ring roller snaffle on page 42). Accordingly, there are alloys that include copper, such as Kangaroo metal, Aurigan, Minos and Cyprium.

Some horses find lightweight, plastic-coated bits comfortable. Happy Mouth bits have a polyurethane outer over a stainless steel core; plastic- or rubber-covered bits without a core can be chewed right through and are therefore not recommended. Nylon is also tough and lightweight.

A wet mouth allows the bit to glide over the bars.

Sweet iron snaffle with copper inlays; both materials encourage salivation.

Rubber can be soft, hardened or vulcanized. Theoretically, hardened and vulcanized rubber is the same, as sulphur or sulphur compounds are added to the rubber, but old vulcanite bits have a different texture from today's hardened rubber ones.

The newest material on the bit market is titanium, which is ultra-lightweight. It is particularly popular in racing, where every ounce counts. Brushed steel is also being promoted as a new material, and manufacturers claim horses like its texture.

Plastic bits and those in a new titanium range offer a choice of colours, which appeals to many young riders. So if you like to think pink – or blue, or purple – and your horse goes well in one of these bits, you can now colour co-ordinate if you want.

A lightweight Happy Mouth bit.

Rubber can be hardened or vulcanized.

Brushed steel mouthpiece with copper lozenge.

TIP

When choosing a rubber- or plastic-coated bit with loose rings, make sure the rings turn freely. They sometimes turn so far, then lock, which negates the bit's action – and if one ring runs freely and the other sticks, you're likely to end up with a one-sided horse.

'Of every twenty bits I make, nineteen are for men's heads and not more than one really for the horse's head.'
Benjamin Latchford, loriner, 1883

CHEEKPIECES FOR SNAFFLES

The design of a bit cheekpiece also affects its action. This applies particularly to the snaffle family, which is the largest and most popular of the groups. See the section on double bridles (pages 50–51) for information on bradoons.

To say that a horse has a 'snaffle mouth' implies that he is easily controlled and responsive, and a snaffle is invariably used to start a horse's education, whatever his future job. Snaffles are also mandatory for some competitions, notably the first levels of dressage, where only certain designs are permitted, and some novice showing classes.

The classic snaffle cheekpieces are D-ring, full cheek, eggbutt, loose ring, and Fulmer loose ring.

D-rings are said to have a slight 'lifting' action on the mouthpiece. Their construction means that the joint of a single-jointed snaffle lies slightly lower on the tongue than with other cheekpieces, which encourages some horses to put their tongues over the bit.

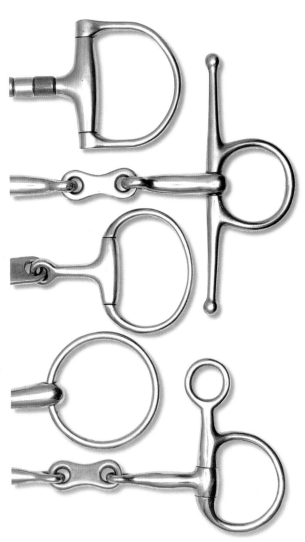

From the top: D-ring, full cheek, eggbutt, loose ring and hanging cheeks. D-rings have a slight lifting action and help keep the bit central, so can be useful for horses who lean or to reinforce steering aids. However, a single-jointed mouthpiece with D-rings hangs lower than with other cheeks, so isn't suitable for horses who try to put their tongues over the bit.

Full cheeks help with steering. Eggbutt cheeks keep the mouthpiece relatively still and central and prevent pinching, so are a good choice for horses who go behind the bit or for riders with unsteady hands. Hanging cheeks apply a small amount of poll pressure and also suspend the mouthpiece, so encourage a round outline and reduce tongue pressure.

Full or spoon cheeks apply gentle pressure and reinforce steering aids. The Fulmer loose ring has full cheeks and a loose ring set outside the mouthpiece, combining steering help with a small amount of play.

Eggbutt cheeks keep the mouthpiece relatively still and the smooth sides minimize the risk of pinching or rubbing. They, like other fixed cheeks, keep the bit central in the mouth and often help with horses who tend to go behind the bit.

Loose rings allow the mouthpiece to make continual small movements in the mouth; they encourage the horse to mouth and discourage him from leaning or setting himself above the bit, but there is a risk of pinching.

A Fulmer loose ring should always be used with leather keepers, which link the bit cheeks to the bridle cheekpieces and keep it at the correct height and angle in the mouth. Full cheeks can be used with or without them: using them keeps the bit less mobile in the mouth.

Fulmer and full cheek snaffles should be designed so the tops of the cheeks bend slightly away from the horse's face. Some modern designs don't allow for this and there is a risk that they can put constant pressure on horses with fleshy or relatively large muzzles, for example, cobs.

Fulmer loose ring snaffles should be used with keepers to keep them at the right height and angle in the horse's mouth. Because the ring is set outside the mouthpiece, the bit hangs too low if keepers aren't used. Full cheek snaffles, where the rings are set on to the mouthpiece, can be used with or without keepers. With keepers, the bit stays very still in the mouth, and without them, there is a small amount of movement.

The sleeve or T-bar snaffle gives the movement of a loose ring with the comfort of an eggbutt.

TIP

Sleeve or T-bar snaffles have long been used in the USA and are now found in some British designs, such as the Wilkie snaffle (see page 36). The loose ring runs through a T-shaped sleeve, thus combining the movement of a loose ring with the comfort of an eggbutt. This is a great idea that should be used more often.

'Simple bits are the best. I always try to use some type of snaffle when possible, though I will often try different ones to find the one in which the horse goes best. To go well, a horse has to be comfortable in his mouth. If they don't accept the bit, they will never allow you to ride them properly and you will never realize their potential.'
Franke Sloothaak (Germany) leading international show jumper

POLL PRESSURE

Many horses and ponies respond well to gentle poll pressure, provided the rider recognizes that, as soon as the horse answers this request to lower his head, the pressure must be released.

The hanging cheek applies a small amount of poll pressure.

All pelhams, kimblewicks and curb bits apply some poll pressure. There are also some snaffles that act on this point – some which are deservedly popular, some of which are misunderstood. All are available with a variety of mouthpieces.

The hanging cheek or Baucher snaffle applies a small amount of pressure and encourages a round outline. As always, a horse can only be on the bit if he is working from behind – lowering his head and tucking in his nose doesn't mean he is working correctly.

If the bit is made correctly, with the mouthpiece set just above the centre of the ring, the cheek tilts as the rein contact is taken up, so poll pressure is activated but pressure on the bars and tongue is reduced. If the mouthpiece is central on the ring, as with some inferior examples, the cheek doesn't tilt and the bit doesn't work as it should.

Myler bits with hooks (slots) are suspended in the mouth and apply a little poll pressure. Cheekpieces described as beval or cartwheel snaffles combine poll pressure with a little mobility in the mouthpiece; these are sometimes said to have a gag action, but this isn't strictly true.

Fastening the cheek to the top slot and the reins to the ring provides a little poll pressure. If the rein is fastened to the second inset ring, the ring slides down and the action is more definite. One version is marketed as the Wilkie snaffle and has a T-bar to prevent pinching.

With the rein on the large ring of a three-ring snaffle, there is some poll pressure but little leverage. When the rein is attached to the second or third rings, the pressure is increased and so is the leverage, and the bit's central joint lifts towards the roof of the mouth. Many people use the third ring position to give them extra brakes – but as shown here, the leverage is considerable and the horse often pulls harder because it is uncomfortable.

The American gag or elevator is misnamed, as it is neither. It has a lowering effect – when the horse doesn't throw up his head to try to avoid the discomfort!

LEVER BITS

Bits with lever cheeks, such as the three-ring snaffle, American gag/elevator and Tom Thumb bit (see Western bits, page 70) are sometimes classed as snaffles, though they don't fit into this category.

All can be seen in use on horses whose riders lack control. Sometimes, all they do is cause discomfort or pain.

Using the large ring on a three-ring bit applies a small amount of poll pressure; using the first small ring applies a little more. Lowering the rein further exerts more leverage and tilts the bit, so the horse inevitably opens his mouth to try to avoid the discomfort.

Some riders use a connecting strap on the large rings to limit the bit's movement, but this is not really satisfactory.

Always use a gag snaffle with two reins.

GAGS

Gag bits should always be used with two reins and, in this way, can be both effective and humane on horses who have learned to put their heads into their chests and go. One rein – the direct rein – attaches to the bit ring in the ordinary way, the other to the running cheeks, which pass through slots in the rings.

Hold the reins as you would those of a double bridle or pelham, with the direct rein as the top, snaffle rein and the gag rein as the bottom one. Alternatively, knot the gag rein and let it rest on the neck until you need to pick it up.

This means you only use the gag rein, which raises the bit in the mouth, when necessary and the horse does not become immune to its action.

PELHAMS AND KIMBLEWICKS

Both of these bits attempt to combine the actions of a double bridle (see pages 50–51) within one mouthpiece. Their action is much less precise, but many horses and ponies go well in them – and because lots of riders find it easier to ride with light hands using a pelham in particular, they can keep both halves of the partnership happy. They are a favourite with showing riders who do not want to use a double bridle, and some top showing riders always make pelhams their first choice.

PELHAMS

Pelhams have small rings at the top to take the bridle cheekpieces, which means the mouthpiece stays relatively still. It also means that by activating the reins a small amount of poll pressure is applied, encouraging the horse to lower his head slightly. The top ring takes the equivalent of the bradoon (snaffle) rein while the bottom takes the curb rein. Pelhams are more effective if used with two reins and with practice this comes easily – if you're worried, try riding with two reins on a snaffle to get the feel of operating them independently.

Using the top rein activates the mouthpiece and slight poll pressure. Using the bottom rein introduces more leverage and also brings the curb chain into action. If you want to use one rein, you need to use pelham roundings: loops which fasten to the top and bottom rings on each side. This gives an action somewhere between that of the top and bottom reins.

Traditionally, a pelham cheekpiece is the same size as the mouthpiece, so a 12.5cm (5in) mouthpiece will have a 12.5cm (5in) cheekpiece. Relatively longer cheeks are capable of more leverage and should be used with care.

TIP

Pelhams are not permitted in dressage competitions run under Fédération Équestre International (FEI) rules, which govern most national dressage organizations, but they can be used in show jumping and cross-country.

Myler pelhams
Mouthpieces from the Comfort snaffle styles are also available with pelham cheekpieces, and horses who go well in the snaffles will often also be receptive to the pelham version.

KIMBLEWICKS

Used with one rein, kimblewicks act, in theory, like a hanging cheek snaffle with the rider's hands held higher, or when the reins are put in the top of two slots found on some cheekpieces. When the hands are lowered or the reins used in the bottom slot they have a slight curb action. In practice, such short cheekpieces are capable of minimum leverage. However, some horses and ponies do respond well to this bit, often because

the most commonly used mouthpiece has a small port which allows room for the tongue.

Variations on a theme

Both pelhams and kimblewicks come with a huge range of mouthpieces. They range from Happy Mouth (see page 40) or rubber-covered, to many of the mouthpieces used in snaffles. The most common are the mullen mouth and mouthpieces with ports of varying sizes. Specialist pelham designs include those examples pictured below.

TIP

Don't feel like a failure if you need to use a bit other than a snaffle for potentially more exciting activities such as hacking and jumping. It is essential to be in control and better to use a potentially stronger bit gently than a theoretically milder one more harshly.

'I back my young horses in a snaffle, but change to a pelham as quickly as possible, because it teaches them to carry themselves from the beginning.'
Lynn Russell, top British showing rider

The Sam Marsh pelham
Named after its inventor, this has a flat mouthpiece with a port and is hinged on each side. It stays in the correct position whatever the angle of the horse's head and can help with those who try to lean on the bit.

The Scamperdale pelham
This has the bottom cheek angled away from the face, to avoid pinching, and to minimize the risk of the horse grabbing it.

The Cambridge mouth kimblewick
This has a small port, which allows room for the tongue.

CURB CHAINS

A component of double bridles, pelhams, kimblewicks, Liverpool driving bits and some Western bits, a curb chain sits in the curb groove at the back of the horse's jaw, where there is a reflex point. When the rein is used in such a way that the curb chain applies light pressure there, the horse is encouraged to relax his jaw.

The action of the curb chain only works if it is fitted correctly. It must be at the right height and right tension and lie flat. Follow these steps:

1. Attach an end link to the offside curb hook and twist it clockwise so that the chain lies flat and the fly link (the loose ring at the centre) is on the bottom edge.

2. With your fingers between the chain and the horse's jaw, hook the last link on to the nearside curb hook. Keep your thumbnail pointing up so the chain lies flat.

3. The chain should touch the horse's jaw when the cheekpiece is drawn back to an angle of 45 degrees. If it is too loose, the cheeks will come too far back; if too tight, the chain will act too soon. In both cases, the horse may be uncomfortable.

4. If you need to shorten the chain, work out which link will take up the slack, and slip it over the nearside curb hook. Keep your thumbnail pointing down and the chain will continue to lie flat.

5. With a kimblewick, pass the chain through the bit rings on each side to encourage it to lie flat and lie in the curb groove without riding up. The same technique can be used with a pelham, passing it through the top bit rings.

If you have ever had problems with fitting a curb chain comfortably, you are probably not alone. Curb chain hooks are remarkably badly designed for something that has been used for so many years! If you can find them, flat hooks are much better, though they are rarely seen for sale. If there is a risk of hooks pressing against a fleshy jaw, try removing them and using an American buckle-on leather curb chain.

Classic curb chains are single or double link, but double link chains offer a wider bearing area and are usually preferred. The central flylink is designed to accommodate a lip strap, which in turn helps to ensure the curb chain lies flat. Many riders don't bother with these, but apart from keeping the curb chain in position, they add a 'finished' look for the show ring.

A lip strap should be loose enough not to come into contact with the jaw, but not so loose it could flap and irritate.

TIP

Sensitive horses may go better in a leather or elastic curb chain. Alternatively you could pass the chain through a rubber or gel sleeve.

AT THE DOUBLE

Double bridles are designed to give subtle communication to educated horses, not to provide extra brakes. A horse should be balanced, responsive and work truly on the bit in a snaffle before being introduced to a double. Also, he must physically have enough room in his mouth for two bits. Horses with short mouths, which includes many cobs, sometimes find double bridles literally too much of a mouthful.

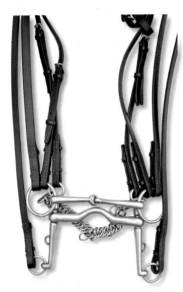

A loose ring bradoon combined with a sliding cheek Weymouth is a classic combination.

Double bridles always comprise a thin snaffle called a bradoon and a curb bit. Each comes in many designs; together, they are sometimes called a Weymouth set, though a Weymouth is actually a particular type of curb.

Most experts recommend using a bradoon 6mm–12mm (¼–½in) longer than the horse's usual snaffle – but make sure it doesn't come too low in the mouth.

So how do you choose the appropriate bradoon and curb? The classic guidelines are that if a horse goes better in bits allowing more 'play', a loose ring bradoon and sliding cheek curb should suit him, but if he tends to come behind the bit, an eggbutt bradoon and fixed cheek curb are more logical.

As always, horses have their own preferences and you may find, for instance, that a loose ring bradoon and fixed cheek curb produce the perfect response.

Bradoons with gag cheeks are sometimes seen in the show ring and on the polo field, but few riders would want or need such overkill.

TIP

Traditionally, bradoons have small ring mouthpieces simply because this looks neater. However, some trainers feel that using one with standard snaffle rings – in other words, a snaffle with a very thin mouthpiece – gives the rider more 'feel'.

A double bridle should be used to give subtle communication to an educated horse.

CHEEK TO CHEEK

Fixed cheek curbs are just that: there is no movement of the mouthpiece. The sliding cheek allows a little movement up and down in the mouth. Finally, there is the Banbury curb, which has a revolving mouthpiece and cheeks that have independent movement – an idea that is not as new as some manufacturers would like us to believe.

The fixed cheek curb gives an instant, definite cue. The sliding cheek is a little more subtle and the horse gets a warning that he is about to be given a signal, which seems a fair and polite way of communicating your intentions. Western-style riders may use 'loose jaw' shanks (cheeks) because of this two-stage action.

The Banbury is actually rather vague... which may be why so many horses like it. The Belton bit, shown on page 53, works on similar principles.

Check the curb's proportions. Because it is a lever, the shorter the proportion of the cheek above the mouthpiece relative to the one below it, the greater the potential leverage. In general, the lower cheek should be twice the length of the upper one.

This combination of Myler bits was recommended by Myler UK clinician Hilary Vernon for a horse with fleshy lips and a large tongue. The bradoon has a French link mouthpiece with slightly angled arms and the forward angled curb has a wide port; both allow room for the tongue. Conventional curb hooks, which could dig into fleshy lips, have been replaced by screw loops available from any hardware or DIY store.

'The decision on when to introduce a double bridle depends on a horse's way of going rather than his age. He must be going forward, accepting a snaffle bridle and engaged behind. I never put one on until I'm happy with the way a horse goes in a snaffle, which has little to do with age.'
Richard Ramsay, show producer and BHSI

FITTING AND INTRODUCING A DOUBLE BRIDLE

When a double bridle is fitted correctly, the bradoon fits snugly into the corners of the mouth without pulling them upwards – unless the horse has particularly fleshy lips – and the curb sits below. The old saying is that the curb should be 2.5cm (1in) above the tushes in a gelding and 5cm (2in) above the corner teeth in a mare.

As with the pelham and kimblewick, the curb chain should come into play when the rein draws back the cheek to an angle of 45 degrees.

The curb comes into play when drawn back to 45 degrees, and the greater the contact taken on the rein, the more leverage is exerted.

TIP

If you've never used a double bridle before, try to have a few lessons with a good trainer on an experienced, well-schooled dressage or showing schoolmaster before attempting to introduce it to your horse. This will give you confidence and dexterity.

To introduce a double bridle or pelham, fit it in the stable and let the horse play with the bits: if necessary, give him a mint or other treat to encourage this. Hold the reins as if you were in the saddle and take a light contact on the bradoon rein, keeping the curb rein loose, then ask him to flex left and right.

Now activate the curb rein lightly, just enough for him to feel its action. Immediately he lowers his head, release it.

Once he accepts this, ride in a safe, enclosed area in walk. Keep the curb rein loose – even the weight of it will send a subtle signal. If he stays relaxed, move forwards to trot, without asking for anything more than large turns and circles.

Your first session should last only about ten minutes and you can then gradually increase the time and questions asked until he is as confident in a double bridle as he is in a snaffle.

Halfway house

Some trainers like to go straight from a snaffle to a double bridle, while others use a pelham with two reins as a halfway house. The Belton bit, designed by Paul Belton of Albion Saddlery in conjunction with German dressage supreme Klaus Balkenhol, was designed as a transition bit and has a mouthpiece similar to the Banbury curb, with a top ring to take the snaffle rein. Introduce your horse to either of these bits as explained above.

Take a light contact and ask the horse to flex.

Start in walk, with a loose curb rein. These photos show a genuine introduction to a pelham and the first time this pony had been ridden in one.

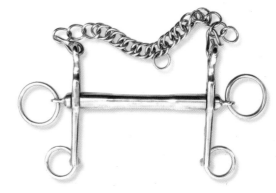

The Belton bit was designed as a halfway house between a snaffle and a double bridle.

WINNING COMBINATIONS

Using nose pressure as a control point is nothing new, but over the past few years riders have become more aware of the benefits of using nose pressure in combination with a bit. It is a logical way of starting a youngster's education, as he will already be used to nose pressure as a control point, having been led in a headcollar, but it can also help with many horses who become strong in certain situations.

Some training systems recommend that early riding should be done using a rope halter or bitless bridle (see pages 74–7) and that a bit should be employed only when the horse can maintain his balance when carrying a rider. However, most riders prefer to use a bit from the start, and a combination bit and noseband that disperses pressure over the nose, poll, mouth and curb groove can be an excellent solution.

The most popular version is probably the Myler combination, which has a rawhide noseband. This gives a clear signal, but some horses may respond better if it is used in conjunction with a sheepskin sleeve.

A single rein is usually attached to the lower ring, but you can use another rein on the large one to give the option of a direct snaffle action.

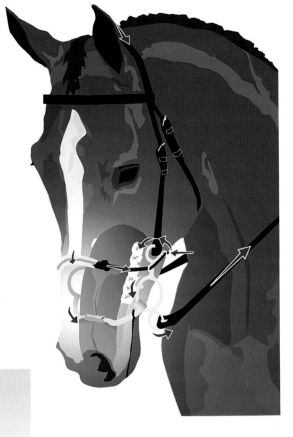

The Myler short-shank combination bit is versatile and kind. It can be used at the start of a horse's education to combine nose pressure – which he will be used to – with the action of the bit and is also effective on strong horses, who tend to pull much less. The reason for this is that control points are dispersed around the nose and mouth, as shown. As with all Myler bits, the mouthpiece allows room for the horse's tongue and does not restrict his swallowing.

The Mikmar combination bit has a lightweight aluminium mouthpiece and is available in several versions, including one with a contoured mouthpiece and another with swivelling cheekpieces said to make it easier to obtain flexion. Most riders – and horses – will be more comfortable with the low-port version.

Again, pressure can be dispersed over the poll, mouth, curb groove and nose, and rein position can be altered according to which control points you wish to emphasize.

The Mikmar combination bit is said to make it easier to lighten the forehand and obtain flexion.

COMBINATION CONFUSION

There has been much confusion and controversy over combination bits. This stems from two misconceptions: one is that they are severe and the other is that they are suited mainly to Western-style riding.

The Myler combination bit is popular with event riders, particularly for the cross-country phase. Critics mistakenly assume it works because they believe it has a severe action – but as I have already explained, it has a relatively mild action because of the variety of control points. Horses do not back off from pain, they pull against it!

If a horse is used to being ridden in a bit and you want to introduce a combination bit, start with the noseband on its loosest setting, so the bit acts first. Introduce the idea of nose, jaw and poll pressure by tightening the jaw strap gradually, a hole at a time, over several minutes so he has time to get used to the action. However, if using a combination bit when backing a young horse, adjust the noseband more tightly so its action takes precedence over the bit's and if you wish, gradually change the emphasis until you can use a bit on its own.

TIP

A simple but effective way to give the option of nose or bit pressure is to use an appropriate snaffle with a drop noseband fastened *above* the bit. Attach one pair of reins to the snaffle rings and another to the side rings of the noseband and hold them as you would the reins of a double bridle.

NEW IDEAS

Every time you think there can't possibly be anything new to put in a horse's mouth, someone invents a bit or system. Whether all new products are true innovations or reinventions of the wheel provokes much discussion.

THE MYLER BIT SYSTEM

Myler bits, developed in the USA by brothers Dale, Ron and Bob Myler, have become hugely popular worldwide in both English and Western-style riding. Their design and use are well thought out, and advocates say that there is a Myler bit for every horse – though to make the right choice from the huge range of mouthpieces and cheekpieces, you may need to get advice from someone trained in their uses and applications and who can preferably see you and your horse work.

The Myler system categorizes bits according to three levels of training, and emphasis is gradually switched to different control points in the mouth and on the head. There are also three key design points: the bits are shaped to allow room for the tongue; joints are protected by barrels (sleeves) to ensure there is no pinching; each side of the mouthpiece can be used independently.

The inventors maintain that this independent side movement allows simpler, clearer signalling. This, they say, may require adjustment in your riding technique, as you can be more subtle in your actions as you ask your horse to bend or lift his shoulder.

Many of the bits have slots at the top and further round the cheeks to take the bridle cheekpiece and reins. Using the top slot gives a little poll pressure; using the rein slot as well adds more.

This Myler snaffle has the range's trademark shaped mouthpiece and independent side movement. The copper roller encourages the horse to relax his jaw and tongue.

THE KY ROTARY SNAFFLE

Also designed as an alternative to the traditional single-jointed snaffle, this has a ball-centre swivel joint, which enables the sides of the bit to rotate independently. Said to eliminate pinching, it offers the rider a more definite 'feel' than a French link, which some people prefer.

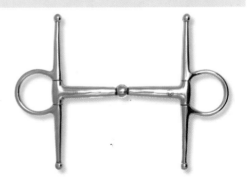

The KY rotary snaffle's ball-centre swivel joint is said to eliminate pinching.

THE PEEWEE BIT

This is a loose ring bit with a sweet iron mullen mouthpiece and angled side-bars that put pressure on the sides of the jaw, not the face. It gives clear signals and can be used in three positions, two with a snaffle action and one that gives the action of a mild curb.

This bit was tried on a variety of horses and ponies for this book; none seemed to dislike it and several showed a noticeable improvement in their way of going. However, the mouthpiece is thin and extra care must be taken to ride with a light hand.

The Peewee bit gives clear signals and can be used in three positions.

THE ROCKIN S BIT

Designed by American horseman Mark Sulan, and a favourite with trainer Mark Rashid for horses with 'bit issues', this is said to disperse pressure via the floating rings. The top ring takes the bridle cheekpieces and gives a degree of poll pressure and the reins attach to the D-rings. You may get a similar effect by using a hanging cheek snaffle with rubber bitguards.

The Rockin S bit is said to disperse pressure via the floating rings.

DENNEY DUAL ACTION BITS

These have two-part cheekpieces incorporating cased springs and are designed to mimic the action of a double bridle with one mouthpiece and one rein. As the rider or driver increases the contact, the springs compress and the curb chain comes into play and as the horse reacts, the curb action is released. The designers are also developing a range of snaffles incorporating the spring system, where its shock-absorbing properties are said to minimize the effects of an unsteady rein contact.

Springs in the Denney Dual Action bit promote a kind, consistent rein contact.

'A bit cannot train your horse. That's your job – just make sure you have the best equipment and knowledge to communicate with him effectively.'
Dale Myler

QUESTIONS AND ANSWERS

Q What's the best bit to use when starting a young horse who has never worn one before? I've been told that old-fashioned breaking bits with keys are no longer popular.

A Different trainers have different ideas, but it's true that breaking bits with keys on the mouthpiece aren't as popular as they once were. The theory is that horses play with the keys, which encourages them to salivate. Unfortunately, this can encourage them to fuss with the bit and may also encourage tongue evasions.

A lightweight, unjointed plastic mouthpiece such as a Nathe or Happy Mouth snaffle is probably the most popular choice. This allows the horse to get used to the feel of something in his mouth, and because it's lightweight, most horses accept it fairly quickly.

An unjointed plastic mouthpiece such as this Happy Mouth snaffle (above) can be a better choice than a traditional breaking bit with keys (top) when introducing a bit.

Q My horse is difficult to load and tries to pull away from the ramp. It's been suggested that I use a Chiffney to give me more control. What is this, and would this work?

A The Chiffney is a potentially severe bit that was originally designed for the racing world, to give more control over colts and stallions prone to rearing. It should never be used for riding and only at all with great caution, as it could inflict a lot of damage on a horse's mouth and jaw.

The shallow, U-shaped section goes into the horse's mouth and puts pressure on the tongue, bars and lips and the rest of the bit encircles the lower jaw. It is usually fitted just with a headpiece, which buckles to the small side rings, while a rope or lunge line clips to the bottom ring.

The idea behind it is that if a horse throws up his head preparatory to rearing, a quick check on the lead rope provides enough of a shock to discourage him, and as soon as he lowers his head, pressure is released. However, if the pressure is not released – or if it causes pain – it may make things worse rather than better.

A better solution would be to get expert help from someone who understands groundwork and can help you teach your horse to load without force, perhaps using a pressure halter or headcollar such as the Dually (see page 101). You also need to make sure that your horsebox or trailer is parked safely, so that the horse has safe footing, that the interior is light and inviting and the ramp is stable.

And, of course, it's vital that whoever drives or tows gives the horse a comfortable journey, with smooth gear changes and no sudden braking or acceleration.

A Chiffney (top) is potentially severe and was designed as an anti-rearing bit. A headcollar such as the Dually (above), combined with groundwork, will be more useful for solving loading problems.

Q My young horse goes best in a loose ring Ultra KK snaffle, but because he is still a bit wobbly, it doesn't always stay central in his mouth. I tried an eggbutt version, but he isn't so relaxed. Is there anything I can do?

A Rubber bitguards, sometimes called biscuits, keep the mouthpiece central and also give very gentle pressure on the sides of the face when turning. If you find that they are difficult to fit over the bit cheeks, soak them in hot water for a few minutes, which makes this much easier.

Alternatively, you could use a leather strap to link the rings behind the jaw, adjusted just tight enough to maintain stability. Unfortunately, neither of these are currently permitted in UK and FEI competition rules.

Rubber bitguards or biscuits help keep a loose ring bit central.

3

BRIDLES

CONTENTS

FITTING BRIDLES

Choosing and fitting a bridle is as important as choosing and fitting a bit, but look in any equestrian magazine and you'll see pictures of ones that are badly adjusted. Sometimes, the horses who are wearing them belong to professionals – this mistake is not exclusive to amateur riders.

The picture below shows the key elements of a well-fitting bridle and how to adjust it. Don't ignore any of these points, or you'll be subjecting your horse to discomfort and possibly setting up problems ranging from resistance to head shaking.

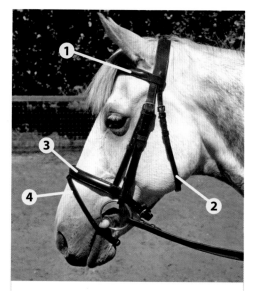

KEY
1. The browband should be long enough to prevent the ears being pinched.
2. There should be four fingers' width between the throatlatch and the horse's face.
3. There should be at least a finger's width between the top of a noseband and the bottom of the facial bones and it should not be so tight it prevents the horse mouthing the bit.
4. There should be at least a finger's width between a drop strap and the horse's muzzle.

The commonest mistakes are browbands that are too short, throatlatches that are too tight and nosebands that are at the wrong height and/or too tight.

A browband that is too short pulls the bridle headpiece on to the base of the ears, causing it to pinch. Horses hate having their ears pinched and may shake or throw their heads about. Some riders then resort to bits with marked poll pressure or tight martingales.

If a throatlatch is too tight it will cause problems when your horse flexes at the poll. If a noseband is positioned too high it will rub the facial bones.

Throatlatches are, in theory, supposed to help prevent the horse's bridle being pulled over his head in a fall, but if they are tight enough to do this, they are far too tight for comfort. At the Spanish Riding School in Vienna, the riders use bridles without throatlatches; perhaps the rest of us should follow suit! A noseband that is too low may, depending on its design, interfere with anything from the action of the bit to the horse's breathing (see page 66).

A correctly adjusted throatlatch allows the horse to flex his jaw.

GETTING THE LOOK

When choosing a bridle, consider whether it actually complements your horse's head. The golden rule is that the heavier or more workmanlike the head, the heavier the weight of the leather should be.

Weight is determined by the width of the cheekpieces, with other parts in proportion. Cobs and other workmanlike types look best with 2cm (¾in) cheekpieces and broad, flat nosebands and browbands; most saddlers still work in Imperial measures.

Horses and ponies with finer heads are suited by 1cm (½in) cheekpieces and, perhaps, nosebands and browbands that are padded and have decorative stitching.

The commonest mistake is to use a lightweight bridle on a heavy head in an attempt to give the illusion of more quality. This will only make your horse look like a football player in a tutu.

To be aesthetically perfect, the buckles of the cheekpieces and the one that adjusts the height of the noseband should be level with each other and with the horse's eyes. To achieve this, you may need to have a bridle made to measure, which is not cheap.

Reins and cheekpieces can be attached to the bit in a variety of ways. Buckles are clumsier but safer than hook stud billets. Clip bridles, also known as work bridles, are especially popular on busy yards. Cheekpieces and, sometimes, reins have clip fastenings, allowing bits to be swapped quickly.

A workmanlike bridle suits a workmanlike head.

Bridles are usually made in Shetland (or extra small), pony, cob, full and extra full sizes. However, the proportions of the head vary between breeds and types, and you may find that you need to mix and match bridle parts in different sizes to get a perfect fit. For instance, a horse with a fine head may need a full size bridle with a cob or even pony size noseband, and a native pony may need a full size browband and noseband with cob size cheekpieces.

Hook stud billets are neater, but not as safe as buckles.

Safety first

Never use a bridle that is so fine it simply isn't strong enough. This may apply to some rolled leather designs, especially those designed for Arabians. Sometimes, thin nosebands are strengthened with metal cores, which makes them potentially severe.

Synthetic bridles have become much more socially acceptable and can be a great option for everyday use, especially in bad weather. Endurance riders often use them in competition, but for other disciplines, good-quality leather is always the first choice.

Make sure that a synthetic bridle has points where, in an emergency, it will break. For instance, if your horse puts his foot through the reins, it's essential that they give way to avoid injury to either of you.

The 'bling' factor

Traditionally, brown leather tack is always used for showing and hunting, while dressage riders prefer black. But if you want to add a bit of bling, you can find pink leather and browbands that are covered with velvet ribbon or have silver, gold or brass inlays – or even Swarovski crystals. In competition, check what's acceptable within your discipline or you'll be noticed, but for the wrong reasons.

Showing, in particular, is a minefield. For instance, while hacks and riding horses are usually shown with velvet-covered browbands, these are never used on cobs or hunters.

Browbands with brass inlays are traditionally the preserve of the driving world, and show jumpers seem to prefer anything with bling!

Velvet-covered browbands are used on show hacks, riding horses and show ponies.

COMFORT ZONES

Bridles such as the Elevator bridle – not to be confused with the severe bit of the same name – and the Albion KB are designed to give extra comfort by dispersing pressure. They take the noseband straps over the headpiece instead of underneath it, thus giving a wider bearing surface, and both the poll area and the front and back of the noseband are padded.

An Albion KB bridle.

'People often come to me for lessons bemoaning the fact that their horse will not go 'on the bit' without a fight. Apart from harsh hands, one of the prime causes I encounter is that many riders do up the throatlatch so tightly that as soon as the horse tries to flex at the poll the strap pulls up into his jowl – and practically throttles him.'
Heather Moffett

ON THE NOSE

Some types of noseband are often used to give the rider more control, but while these can be very useful, they can sometimes cause more problems than they solve. If you think you need more help because your horse opens his mouth or sets his jaw to evade the rein aids, check his mouth and teeth, and your riding.

One school of thought holds that if you use a noseband that fastens above and below the bit, it will only come into effect when necessary. But some horses are unhappy with any form of restriction round the mouth and jaw and may be easier to ride when this is removed.

So why use a noseband at all? Western-style riders usually don't use them, because neck reining doesn't set up mouth resistances: there's a lesson there for the rest of us. And if you're riding a young horse who is teething, some nosebands may put pressure on sensitive areas.

However, if you want your horse's head to have a 'finished' look, a cavesson noseband, which fastens above the bit, completes the picture. When it's fastened, you should be able to fit at least two fingers between it and the horse's face.

Western-style riders usually don't use nosebands on their horses.

DOUBLING BACK

International dressage rules state that double bridles should always be used with cavesson nosebands, and this must be the general recommendation. Crank nosebands, which fasten so tightly they can interfere with jaw flexion, are sometimes used, sadly, even at top level.

Crank nosebands owe their invention to a hard-pulling show cob called Grandstand. His owner, the late Keith Luxford, was a well-known saddler and invented a broad, flat noseband with a doubleback rear fastening that could be tightened more than a standard cavesson.

However, the doubleback fastening is in itself a great idea and is used on pressure-relief bridles such as the Elevator and Albion KB.

Most English-style riders feel a cavesson noseband adds a finished look to a horse's head.

The next step up from a cavesson is a Flash noseband, named after the show jumper it was invented for. It was designed so that a standing martingale could be fixed to the top, cavesson part, while the bottom strap helped to prevent the horse from opening his mouth too far.

Many Flash nosebands are badly designed, with flimsy cavesson parts that pull down the horse's face in use. This means that the bottom strap moves down the horse's mouth and also loosens. To work properly, a Flash noseband must have a substantial cavesson, as shown here, and should be adjusted so that you can easily fit at least one finger between the bottom strap and the horse's muzzle.

Flash converters – butterfly-shaped pieces of leather with a slit in each end that fit over a cavesson noseband and take a bottom strap – allow you to get the action of a Flash without buying a new noseband.

Safety first
A noseband that fastens below the bit should only be used to prevent the horse opening his mouth too far. It should not be used to keep his mouth shut – there is a real difference.

The Elevator Flash noseband has a substantial, padded cavesson.

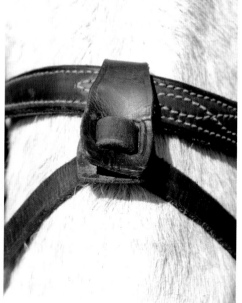

A Flash converter.

'A Flash noseband can be useful in helping to keep the bit central in the horse's mouth.'
Jennie Loriston-Clarke, international dressage rider and trainer

DROP ZONES

The drop noseband is a classic and much-maligned piece of tack that has variously been in and out of fashion. It is said to have been first used, and possibly invented, by the Spanish Riding School, whose training philosophy held that young horses should start their education in a Fulmer loose ring snaffle and drop noseband and progress to a double bridle.

The reasoning behind this is that a correctly fitted drop noseband can help to ask for a lower head position. When a horse opens his mouth, it creates a pressure point low on the nose, coupled with pressure in the curb groove, and as soon as the horse relaxes his jaw and drops his nose, the pressure ceases.

Unfortunately, there are a lot of badly designed and badly adjusted drop nosebands to be seen. They are often made so that the straps that fasten behind the jaw are too short, which in turn means they are adjusted too low and restrict the horse's breathing.

The front of the noseband should rest on the facial bones, because if it lies on the soft, fleshy part below it will interfere with the expansion of the nostrils as the horse breathes. When the horse is standing still, you should be able to fit two fingers between the noseband and his face.

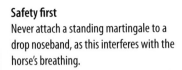

Safety first
Never attach a standing martingale to a drop noseband, as this interferes with the horse's breathing.

A correctly fitted drop noseband.

CROSSING POINTS

Grakle nosebands – named after a hard-pulling Grand National winner. and also known as crossover or figure-of-eight nosebands – are designed to dissuade horses who cross their jaw to pull. Grakles have a less definite pressure point than a drop noseband, so it's often a case of finding out which design a horse responds to best.

The top straps of the standard English Grakle fasten just below the cheekbones, while those of the high ring or Mexican Grakle fasten higher up the face. In both cases, the padded leather disc at the crossover point should rest on the centre of the horse's face.

Some horses resent a standard Flash or Grakle, but respond well to a design that incorporates elastic sections with a small amount of 'give'.

Logic dictates that nosebands that act in the curb groove, which includes all those that fasten above and below the bit, should not be used with bits that incorporate a curb chain – if they are, the action of both becomes confused.

However, you will sometimes see top show jumping and event riders using Flash and Grakle nosebands with pelhams and double bridles. If you're tempted to follow their example, first ask yourself if you also have their riding ability!

The high ring or Mexican Grakle doesn't press on the cheek teeth.

The Barnsby FTS Grakle incorporates elasticated sections, offering a little 'give'.

'I like a Mexican Grakle for young horses who are changing their teeth. It gives that bit more control, but doesn't press on the cheek teeth.'
John Whitaker, international show jumper

CONTROL STRATEGIES

Not all nosebands designed to give extra control rely on restricting the extent to which a horse can open his mouth. Some rely on nose pressure, whereas others are said to have a psychological effect.

KINETON OR PUCKLE NOSEBAND

The Kineton or Puckle noseband comprises two U-shaped metal loops that fit behind the bit rings. When a contact is taken on the reins, pressure is transferred to the nose and the side of the mouth.

Its inventor, the amazingly named Pelham C Puckle, recommended that it should only be used with a mullen mouth snaffle, not a jointed one or with any form of curb bit. When used with a mullen mouth snaffle, pressure is applied to the nose before the bit comes into action – so the horse is given a warning to slow down before a more severe command is applied.

WORCESTER NOSEBAND

The Worcester noseband appeared around the late 1990s in the UK and is still available; it isn't one of the better-known nosebands, but has several useful applications. It works on a combination of bit and noseband pressure, but because the straps, which attach to the rings, limit the backward action of the mouthpiece, it is theoretically milder than a Kineton.

Because it keeps the bit at the correct height in the mouth, it can help with horses who put their tongues over the bit and/or dislike tongue pressure, two tendencies that often go together. It should only be used with some form of snaffle.

The Kineton or Puckle noseband has metal loops that go behind the bit rings.

The Worcester noseband works on a combination of bit and noseband pressure.

The Australian cheeker is believed to have a psychological effect.

Some riders believe the sheepskin noseband encourages a horse to lower his head.

So can you gain extra control over a horse who is too onward bound without using more pressure? A lot of racehorse trainers believe so, which is why the Australian cheeker and the sheepskin noseband are so popular; the latter has also migrated to the fields of eventing and show jumping.

Australian cheeker

The Australian cheeker is a pair of rubber bitguards joined by a central strap. The strap runs up the centre of the horse's face and is fastened to the bridle headpiece.

Obviously, a strip of rubber can't exert any pressure – though this piece of equipment does ensure that the bit doesn't drop too low in the horse's mouth and so helps to relieve tongue pressure. Advocates believe that it works because the horse backs off from the sight of the centre strap running down his face.

Sheepskin nosebands

Sheepskin nosebands, which are actually sheepskin sleeves that fit over a standard cavesson noseband, are said to encourage a horse who holds his head too high to lower it. The theory is that he can't see over the fluffy barrier without dropping his nose, and it is a favourite ploy when horses jump with their heads up and backs flat rather than making a round bascule over a fence.

A sheepskin noseband is sometimes called a shadow roll, as it is also supposed to prevent racehorses shying from shadows on the racetrack.

It has to be said that the jury is still out on whether these nosebands work or just make their users feel better – and it will probably remain there.

WESTERN-STYLE DESIGNS

To English-style riders, some Western-style curb bits may seem severe. In unskilled hands, they can certainly live up to this reputation, but in educated hands, on an educated horse, they can allow fingertip control. The big question is: do you and your horse meet these criteria?

The traditional way of educating a horse was to use a series of bitless bridles with rope nosebands, called bosals. These operate a sophisticated pressure and release control system to which some strongly marketed 'modern' training systems owe a great debt.

As the training progressed, a light bosal was used in conjunction with a curb bit. Finally, the curb bit was used alone.

The other part of the equation is that accomplished Western-style riders rely on shifts in their weight coupled with neck-reining

– any pressure on the bit is very light and sometimes comes only from the weight of the reins.

Many Western-style trainers now prefer to start a young horse in a sidepull, where the reins are attached to rings on the side of the face. It is similar to a scawbrig (see bitless bridles, page 74). They then go to a snaffle, and finally to a curb.

Western-style curbs can have ported mouths or be jointed; it's open to debate whether a jointed Western-style bit is a curb or a lever snaffle. The general recommendation is that a curb with short shanks (cheeks) is the natural first progression from a snaffle.

A shank that swivels is usually regarded as kinder than a fixed shank, as the horse receives a signal that he is about to get a command. In a highly trained horse, that first signal may be all that is needed.

As with English-style bits, there is a variety of mouthpiece designs and materials available. Sweet iron and copper are popular, as they encourage salivation.

TIP

Even when your horse is going nicely and calmly in a curb, it's best to go back to a sidepull or snaffle when you introduce new movements. This ensures that if he is confused about what you are asking, there is less risk of causing him pain or discomfort.

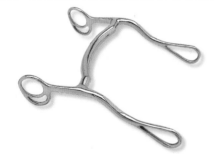

This Western-style bit, from the Toklat range, has a mullen mouth which allows room for the tongue and relatively straight shanks, offering clear communication and comfort.

Western-style show bits often have ornate details on the shanks.

BRIDLES AND REINS

Western-style bridles range from the functional to parade bridles incorporating silver inlays, embossed and engraved leather, and other decorative details. They can have either a browband or a loop that fits over one ear.

Reins are usually heavier than English-style ones, the idea being that the extra weight gives a refined signal through the bit as the rider neck-reins. The two common designs are split reins, with a separate rein attached to each side of the bit, or closed romal reins, with a piece of leather at the end that acts as an encouraging aid, either to the horse or to the cattle being driven. If you've seen cowboy films where riders flip the rein ends from side to side to get their horses to go faster, you've seen romal reins in action. They are the inspiration for the 'modern' wip wop or over and under (see page 127).

As this horse and rider prepare to come to a sliding stop, the split reins can be seen clearly.

A one-ear Western-style bridle with a single loop instead of a browband. There may be less risk of pressure on the ears, but there may also be less security.

Western-style show/parade halters and bridles are beautifully ornate.

REIN OPTIONS

Choosing reins involves more than getting a grip. They need to be the right length, the right width and with more or less bulk to suit individual preferences, as well as being suitable for a particular job.

Reins are made in lengths for ponies and horses. If they are too long, there is a danger that the rider may catch a foot in the loop, and if they are too short, you won't have enough room for adjustment.

Those that buckle on to the bit are safer than billet (hook stud) fastenings but are not as neat. Some showing riders still use reins that are stitched to the bits of a double bridle, as this gives the neatest appearance of all.

WHICH MATERIALS?

Different types of material have individual pros and cons. Classic plain leather reins are smart, and give great communication when supple, but become slippery when wet. Laced and plaited leather gives improved grip, though plaited leather can stretch.

You'll find that when you're using double reins with a pelham or double bridle, you need to minimize bulk, so leather is best for practicality and appearance. The top (snaffle) rein should be wider than the bottom (curb) one to make manipulating them easier, but if you prefer, you can use laced or plaited leather for the top rein for greater security.

Rubber-covered reins give great grip, but can be bulky. Half-rubber or 'dressage reins' with a rubber grip on the inside look smarter and give

grip without bulk, but cheaper designs soon fray at the edges.

Continental web reins have leather handgrips along their length. Some riders like these because they are lightweight and others dislike them for the same reason. You may find that they don't have enough handgrips and/or that they are spaced too far apart to give a fine enough adjustment.

New ideas

Materials borrowed from the car manufacturing industry give good gripping qualities while maintaining flexibility. Alcantara, a man-made material, looks and feels like suede but is much harder wearing, and some manufacturers use it instead of rubber.

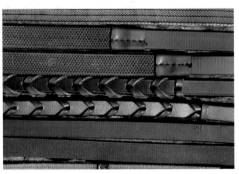

Synthetic, rubber grip, laced, plain and Continental web reins.

Alcantara is a modern alternative to rubber.

Another idea has proved useful for teaching and is popular with children. Reins with multi-coloured grips mean that the pupil can be told to keep their adjustment within a particular colour band. However, it's important to make sure they aren't too bulky for small hands.

Parelli reins with rein leathers, said to act as a counterbalance.

Multi-coloured reins are fun and practical.

Some trainers believe that reins made from yachting rope give the best communication. Followers of the Parelli system recommend rein leathers: leather pendants with slots to take rope reins. These clip to the bit and act as a counterbalance to indicate a signal is about to be given as soon as the reins are picked up.

TIP

Side-saddle riders usually carry their hands further from the horse's mouth than astride riders, so need reins that are longer than standard. Some riders also prefer to use slightly longer reins for cross-country, as this allows them to knot the end near the buckle; this means the reins are less likely to be pulled through the hands, but can be 'slipped' over a drop fence if necessary. However, the Mailer bridging rein is a better alternative (see page 120).

Side-saddle riders need longer reins because they sit further away from the horse's head.

GOING BITLESS

Bitless bridles have come full circle. They were, of course, the original way of controlling a ridden horse, and in the seventh century, the hackamore developed as part of a logical training system. In modern times, they became a second-best alternative when a horse could not or would not accept a bit – and now, for some riders, they have become a preferred option.

WHAT'S IN A NAME?

The terms 'hackamore' and 'bitless bridle' are often interchanged. Strictly speaking, the word 'hackamore' is a variation on 'la jaquima', a training system that uses a series of nose-control bridles before graduating to a curb bit.

Although most trainers introduce a bit right from the start, it makes sense to begin with the control points a horse is used to from being led so that he can find his balance under saddle without damaging the sensitivity of his mouth. Parelli enthusiasts do just this, though they didn't invent the idea.

Logically, you can then move to a combination bit that works on the nose and curb groove first and the mouth second (see pages 54–5) and finally to a bit on its own. Some riders, of course, remain bitless by choice.

This hackamore from the Myler range can be used for either Western or English riding and is particularly suited to disciplines where tight turns are required, such as barrel racing or jumping. Designed by American trainer Neil Merrill, it has hinged cheeks that allow the bridle headstall to stay flat to the face even when a definite leading rein is used, thus giving a clear signal while ensuring the horse's comfort.

KEEP IT SIMPLE

If you want to experiment with riding bitless, the simplest way is to attach reins to the rings of a drop noseband, though this isn't wholly satisfactory as it may slip to the side. The simplest true bitless bridles are the scawbrig and the sidepull.

The scawbrig comprises a strap with rings at each end at the front of the nose and a backstrap that goes through the rings and connects to the reins, thus giving pressure on the nose, the sides of the face and the jaw.

The sidepull, which originated in the USA, is basically a headcollar with rings at the side to take the reins; many have rope sections at the front to give a more definite pressure. One

A synthetic scawbrig bridle.

version designed by American trainer Diana Thompson has small linking straps from the cheekpieces to the noseband to give stable, clear control points.

Monty Roberts's Dually halter (see page 101) can also be used for riding and has the same action as a sidepull.

The next step up is the Blair's pattern bridle, often called the English hackamore. This has a curb strap or chain and metal arms that transfer rein pressure to the nose, jaw and poll.

Finally, there is the potentially severe device usually called a German hackamore. In the right hands, this can give excellent results and some riders show jump and even go cross-country at top level using one. But don't make the mistake of thinking all bitless bridles are mild – the German hackamore has long arms and a curb chain and can exert tremendous pressure and leverage if used incorrectly.

Dr Cook's design

American veterinarian Dr Robert Cook believes that a bit is an impediment to a horse, not only because it can cause pain but because by causing chewing and salivation it interferes with breathing and stride patterns. He has developed a bitless bridle that spreads pressure over a wide area and is said to allow the rider to give a nudge to one side of the face for steering and to 'hug' the head for stopping.

Even if you disagree with his views on bits, Dr Cook's bitless bridle has won a lot of converts, both human and equine.

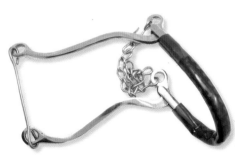

The English hackamore does not have the leverage of the German version (below).

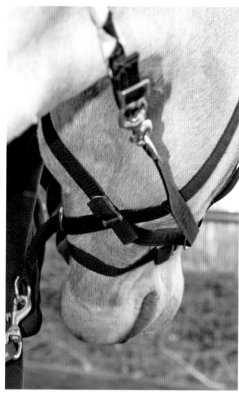

Dr Cook's bitless bridle is designed to hug the head.

FITTING AND USING BITLESS BRIDLES

While most horses and ponies, and their riders, can adapt well to going bitless, it's important that bitless bridles are fitted correctly. They must be adjusted so that there is no risk of the front parts impinging on the soft part of the lower nose and restricting the horse's breathing, and if you are using a bridle all the time, you may need to raise or lower it just a hole occasionally to prevent rubs or calluses forming on the nose.

With English and German hackamores, a common mistake is to fasten them too loosely. As a rule of thumb, they should act on the nose and jaw when the lever arms are at an angle of 45 degrees. In particular, if the jaw strap – or, as with some models, chain – is too loose, the nose pressure will come in too suddenly.

In theory, anything a horse can do wearing a bit, he can do without one. In fact, some riders say they get far better results and far happier horses this way. However, it is a case of looking at each partnership individually, as there are too many factors – including rider ability, horse conformation and soundness and the horse's previous experiences – to be able to say that one method or the other is good or bad.

A competent rider can certainly school a horse to go 'on the bit' without one – though, of course, it would be more accurate to use the phrase 'on the bridle' or 'on the aids'. A true round outline, where the horse steps through from behind, lifts his abdominal muscles and is light in the hand, does not depend on or need contact with a bit.

However, you do need to keep a few things in mind when riding bitless. For a start, begin in a safe, enclosed area so that you and your horse can get used to the approach, and do get help from someone who understands how to fit the bridle correctly and can help you fine-tune your riding technique.

Most of us who ride using a bit place too much emphasis on rein aids, so riding bitless can be a salutary experience even if only done as an experiment.

This English hackamore is adjusted so that when the cheeks are drawn back to 45 degrees, the noseband puts pressure on the front of the face and the jaw.

Happy and relaxed on a Parelli halter.

Event rider Ruth Edge riding Two Thyme in the show jumping phase of a World Cup qualifier using an English hackamore.

Western riders use minimal rein contact and research says horses ridden Western-style are more relaxed.

'Ride as you would normally, with a consistent contact and staying relaxed through your wrists and arms. If the horse stays soft and happy, keep your hands still, but if he gets rigid in the neck, open your hands and play with the reins a little to encourage him to soften – just as you would normally.

Don't get worried by the fact that you're riding with a bitless bridle. The horse won't!

Riding bitless means thinking ahead, being aware of your weight aids and – especially when jumping – asking the horse to turn earlier than you would if you were using a bit. On turns, a neck-reining technique gives good results: bring your outside hand to the neck so it is in line with the crest, not across it, and open your inside hand from the wrist, not the elbow. Keep your elbows at your side so you stay stable and keep the softness through your arms.'

Barrett Watson, show jumping and eventing trainer

QUESTIONS AND ANSWERS

Q My horse is a head shaker when under any form of pressure, such as when he is asked to work on the bit. It doesn't seem to be related to pollen allergy or insect irritation, and my vet has eliminated mouth or teeth problems as a possible cause. I've been told a change of tack can help in some cases – is this true?

A If your horse is head shaking – making quick, jerky movements of the head when ridden, coupled in severe cases by striking out with a foreleg – there are a number of strategies to try. First, as you have already done, it's important to get him checked by your vet and to try to eliminate physical problems.

Check the fit of your bridle and make sure that the browband isn't too short. If it is pulling the headpiece forward on to the base of his ears, this can cause irritation and pinching, which can set off head shaking in some horses.

If you haven't tried a nose net (see page 166) this is also worth doing, even though you say your problems don't seem to be related to pollens or insects. Climate change means that pollens are being dispersed and insects are about at unprecedented times of the year.

It would also be worth trying him in a bitless bridle, preferably one that does not apply poll pressure, such as a scawbrig, sidepull or Dr Cook's. Anecdotal evidence suggests that the Dr Cook's bitless bridle has helped resolve some cases of head shaking, particularly those where there seems to be a psychological element.

Research has also shown that horses who are ridden Western-style, with a longer outline, and who are neck-reined rather than ridden on a contact, are less likely to weave than those ridden English-style. As your horse's behaviour seems to be related to pressure, you may want to try this as a short- or long-term approach and, if you want to return to English-style riding, get expert help to make sure you are not asking more than he is capable of.

Q I've seen show jumpers using small sheepskin sleeves on their bridle cheekpieces and both riding and driving competitors using ear covers on their horses even when there are no insects about. What's the reason for this?

A Both ideas are often seen at big indoor shows, where the arenas are relatively small compared to outdoor shows and the large crowds are 'on top' of the horses. Some riders believe that the small sheepskin sleeves encourage the horse to look ahead, rather than being distracted by what is around him, thus acting as a modified form of blinkers. Blinkers themselves are not allowed under FEI rules and there is some controversy over the use of sleeves.

Some horses are worried by noisy crowds and loudspeakers, particularly indoors, where acoustics often create an echo. Plugging a horse's ears with cotton wool and keeping it in place with fly protectors may help to deaden the noise.

Q I want to show my three-year-old in-hand and have introduced him to a straight-bar plastic snaffle. I've been told I should use a pelham or double bridle in the ring, but am worried this could spoil his mouth.

A Some producers use doubles or pelhams to show big three-year-olds in hand, but there is a huge risk of ending up with a horse who has an unresponsive mouth and is one-sided, owing to more pressure being put on the left-hand side of his mouth.

It is far better to use a snaffle with a coupling that attaches to the bit rings and to the noseband, which gives you two control points and avoids undue pressure on the mouth.

Before you teach him to run up in hand in a bridle, do some groundwork in a control headcollar or halter so he understands what you want him to do without you having to use bit pressure.

4

MARTINGALES & BREASTPLATES

CONTENTS

STABLE INFLUENCES

Although martingales and breastplates have different functions, they have one important thing in common. They can be valuable safeguards and act as a way of preventing a problem, but can't be the sole means of eliminating it. A martingale gives extra control to the rider by coming into action when the horse raises his head too high. It shouldn't be thought of as something that keeps the horse's head down.

Similarly, a breastplate or breastgirth helps to keep a saddle stable, in particular, when the horse is travelling and jumping at speed. This is why it is often regarded as a standard piece of equipment for event horses that are going cross-country, or for racehorses over fences.

What it can't do is turn a badly fitting saddle that moves about too much into one that remains stable. It will act as a back-up on a horse whose saddle has been adjusted as well as possible, and is particularly useful on one whose conformation predisposes him to the saddle moving back.

Breastplates and breastgirths can be used alone, or you can buy martingale attachments that allow you to combine both pieces of equipment without extra bulk.

A breastplate or breastgirth is often standard equipment for fast work.

CHOOSING AND FITTING MARTINGALES

If you've decided to use a martingale, either to give extra control or because you are riding in a situation where you think it would be a sensible precaution, make sure there are still times when you school on the flat, in a safe area, without one.

The reason for this is that, while a martingale can be valuable, it can also lull you into a false sense of complacency, and if you are aiming to compete in dressage competitions, where using one is not permitted, even for warming up, you need to make sure you're confident going without it.

STANDING ROOM

The simplest design is the standing martingale, which attaches to the girth at one end and to a cavesson noseband (or the cavesson part of a Flash) at the other. At one time, most trainers would use it as standard on a young horse; it then went out of fashion, but is now enjoying renewed popularity.

The advantage of a standing martingale is that because it is not linked to the reins, it can't interfere with the horse's mouth. Instead, it works on the nose, which is a control point that horses are introduced to from the first time they are led on a headcollar.

Some people believe that horses can set themselves against a standing martingale and hollow their backs, building up muscle on the underside of the neck instead of along the top. However, this rarely happens unless it is adjusted too tightly, and if a horse does fight against it, you can either switch to a running or bib martingale or ask your saddler to add an insert made from strong elastic so that a little 'give' is incorporated.

A standing martingale cannot interfere with the horse's mouth.

It should be fitted so that when attached to the noseband, it can be pushed up to follow the line of the horse's throat. The neckstrap should be adjusted to allow a hand's width between it and the horse's neck, and a rubber stop must be fitted at the junction of both parts to prevent the martingale dangling between the horse's front legs.

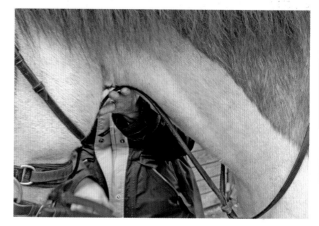

Standing and jumping

It is often advised that a standing martingale should not be used when jumping in case it restricts a horse's head carriage. However, if the horse has a normal jumping style and the martingale is adjusted correctly, this can't happen.

Although a horse raises his head slightly on the approach to a fence, the martingale should not come into play, and when he is moving through the air, his head should come forwards and down, not up.

'I always use a standing martingale when I'm breaking youngsters. When you're leading them in a headcollar you can teach them that a little 'bump' on the headcollar rope means "Come back to me and rebalance yourself" and so if a standing martingale comes into play, it gives a signal they understand.'
Julia Woods, specialist producer of native ponies

RUNNING MARTINGALE

The running martingale is the most frequently used type and, because the reins pass through its rings, has a direct effect on the horse's mouth. This means particular care must be taken with its adjustment – a lot of riders fit it too tightly, which means there is constant pressure on the bars of the mouth.

The standard method of fitting a running martingale is to take back both of the rings and adjust the length at the girth so that they reach the withers. However, if a horse has a particularly sloping or particularly straight shoulder, this can mean that the martingale ends up respectively being either too short or too long.

To get a more accurate fitting, take the rings along the underside of the horse's neck and adjust the martingale so that the rings reach the gullet. If in doubt, have it a little loose rather than a little tight: with a rider on board and the reins held so there is a straight line from the rider's elbow to the horse's mouth, there should not be a kink in the reins where the martingale rings lie.

'I use loose running martingales on all the horses when clients try them, even if they don't need them. It seems to give riders a sense of security when they're on a horse they don't know and the neckstrap is like a comfort zone – especially on cobs with hogged manes.'
Emma Hinckley, show jumper and dealer

Rubber stops must be fitted at the neckstrap junction and on the reins. Never risk leaving off the rein stops, because a ring might catch on the rein fastening or, perhaps even more dangerous, on some designs of bit cheeks.

Pros and cons

Some people are put off by the fact that a running martingale acts directly on the reins, but this can be positive rather than negative. Novice or unskilled riders lack balance and have unsteady hands, but a running martingale helps to minimize unintentional movements of the reins – especially if the horse is ridden in a bit that stays still in the mouth, such as, an eggbutt snaffle.

A running martingale is usually used with a snaffle, but if it has to be used with a pelham or double bridle, logic dictates that the rings should be threaded on to the bottom (curb) rein rather than the top (snaffle) one. This is because a snaffle tends to have a raising action, whereas a curb has a lowering one.

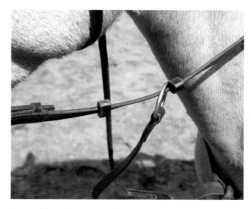

Two rubber stops on each rein.

> **TIP**
>
> A lot of event riders use two rubber stops on each rein, so that they can control the martingale's travel in each direction.

BIB MARTINGALE

The bib martingale is a variation of the running version, where the straps are joined together by a triangular piece of leather. It prevents a horse grabbing the straps and possibly getting a ring hooked up on a tooth and, because the linking triangle puts more weight on the reins and holds them together, it exerts potentially more leverage on the bit.

Because it encourages a lower head carriage, it can give extra control over a strong horse and it is popular with many racing trainers. Its major disadvantage is that it limits the extent to which the rider can open the rein.

Breastplates can have martingale attachments, as with this running martingale and Devoucoux Kolibri breastplate combination.

VARIATIONS ON A THEME

The Market Harborough, Irish martingale and Harbridge or French martingale are all variations on the martingale theme.

Market Harborough

Of the three, the Market Harborough, which is really a cross between a running martingale and a rein, is the most logical and useful.

It fastens to the girth, passes between the front legs and divides into two narrow straps or cords, each with a small clip at the end. The straps then pass through the bit rings and clip on to special reins with small D-rings along their length.

When the horse raises his head too high, the Market Harborough exerts pressure through the rein. The moment he lowers his head, the pressure ceases. It should be fitted fairly loosely to start with, so that the horse gets used to its action, and gradually adjusted so it is at its most effective.

The ordinary (direct) rein buckled to the bit must come into action before the Market Harborough, so it must not be too tight. Unfortunately, it is often labelled as severe simply because it is effective on horses who put their heads in the air to pull or buck, but most horses accept it easily and it can break the vicious circle of a horse and rider pulling at each other.

A lot of trainers use it to re-school older horses who have never been taught to go correctly, and it is often helpful with ex-racehorses. It can also be used when jumping and is popular with producers of children's ponies who are trying to build up correct musculature on small ponies.

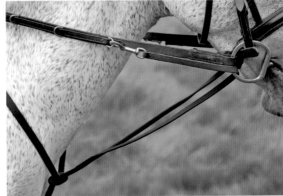

When a pony is too small to be ridden by an adult, and tiny riders don't have the length of leg to school them, a Market Harborough used under experienced supervision can help get results without putting pony or child under pressure.

Harbridge

The Harbridge has the same aim as the running martingale – to discourage the horse from raising his head above the angle of control. It attaches to the bit rings rather than working via the reins, so its action is much more direct. However, the elasticated inserts allow a certain amount of give. It should not be used when jumping, as it could be too restrictive.

Confusingly, at least one British saddler offers a similar design and calls it a French martingale. This name is generally accepted to refer to a design of dog collar and leash with a limited 'choke' action.

Irish martingale

The Irish martingale is usually used only in racing. It's simply a short strap with a ring at each end through which the reins pass, and the idea is that if a jockey falls, it prevents the reins from flying over the horse's head and possibly tripping him up when he's travelling at full speed.

'I often use a Market Harborough on young horses, because if they try to throw up their heads and take off, it tells them that this isn't a good idea! Because the horse works it, not the rider's hands, it rewards him the minute he answers his action and means you don't get into an argument.'
Kate Jerram, specialist in producing young competition and show horses

BREASTGIRTHS AND BREASTPLATES

If you need extra help to prevent a saddle slipping back, or security when jumping at speed, a breastplate or breastcollar/breastgirth can be the answer. It will be even more effective if used in conjunction with a 'grippy' numnah (see page 22).

So what's in a name? The term 'breastplate' is often applied universally, but really belongs to the classic English hunting breastplate. Western designs are similar, but are usually known as breastcollars. In English-style riding, breastcollar or breastgirth are the names usually given to designs with a leather, web or elastic strap that passes round the horse's chest.

PROS AND CONS

The English breastplate comprises a yoke that follows the line of the shoulder and has a connecting strap passing over the withers. It fastens to the girth and to the D-rings of the saddle, via straps running from the yoke.

Its main disadvantage is that D-rings can sometimes pull out. Also, if the saddle isn't the correct width and profile for the horse, the breastplate may stop it sliding back, but will also jam the points of the tree into the sides of the withers, potentially causing severe damage.

The breastcollar comprises a strap that runs round the front of the horse's chest and fastens to one of the girth straps at each side. This immediately makes it more secure than the hunting breastplate and it also has a strap that passes over the withers and keeps it at the correct height.

Its disadvantage is that it is more difficult to fit it correctly and if it is too high, it can impinge on the horse's windpipe and restrict his breathing.

The breastgirth is very similar, though it doesn't have a strap over the withers. It usually fastens to the girth straps, but some designs fasten to the saddle D-rings.

All designs should be fitted with great care – a lot of people adjust them too tightly and restrict the movement of the horse's shoulders, his breathing, or both. As a rule of thumb, a breastplate should be adjusted so that you can fit a hand's width between it and the horse at the chest and the withers, and a breastcollar should run horizontally from the girth round the chest.

NEW IDEAS

New ideas attempt to overcome the disadvantages of traditional breastplates. Two of the most successful are the Kolibri and the FTS FreeFlow breastplate.

The Kolibri, developed by French manufacturers Devoucoux with international event rider Pippa Funnell, is said to combine the actions of a breastplate and a breastcollar without restricting the horse's movement: it has five attachment points to the saddle, five adjustment points and two sliding elastic harnesses to allow freedom of the shoulder.

The Barnsby FTS FreeFlow breastplate incorporates a free-running elastic insert that keeps the tension at the girth adjustment secure, but again, allows the horse's shoulders freedom of movement. This is something event riders and show jumpers are particularly aware of – strangely, most racing trainers seem reluctant to try anything other than traditional designs.

Elasticated breastgirth with running martingale attachment.

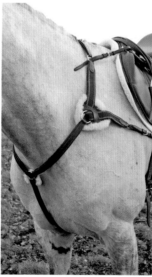

The Devoucoux Kolibri breastplate.

The Barnsby FTS FreeFlow breastplate.

'When I'm backing a young horse and introduce a roller to get him used to the idea of something fastened round his belly, I always use a breastgirth. It means you can adjust the roller just tight enough to keep it in place and know that it won't slip back – something which would frighten a lot of young horses.'
Kate Jerram

QUESTIONS AND ANSWERS

Q I've got a lovely ex-racehorse who I'm hoping to reschool as an all-rounder. He's being well behaved in all respects, but when I hack him out, he throws his head up and down when we're on the way home. I've had his teeth and back checked and there is nothing to worry about, so how can I break this habit?

A This is a habit frequently seen in horses who have come out of racing, and probably starts when they are tired and/or ridden by riders with less than sympathetic hands. Also, some yards pay little attention to the fit of horses' bits and put any bridle on any horse. Racehorses are invariably ridden in loose ring, single-jointed snaffles, so try something different: French link snaffles often suit the typical Thoroughbred mouth conformation better. If you use one with eggbutt or full cheeks, it will stay still in the mouth and encourage the horse to accept it rather than show signs of resistance.

A running martingale will help keep the bit stable, and if he's snatching the reins out of your hands, it's worth using a Mailer bridging rein (see page 120). If this doesn't work, a standing martingale may be more successful.

Resist the temptation to take a stronger contact on the reins, and concentrate on lots of transitions when you're schooling, to help improve his balance.

A running martingale and eggbutt French link snaffle may be a good combination for a horse who throws his head up and down.

Q After learning to ride Western and having enjoyed competing in pleasure classes with my seven-year-old Quarter Horse, I want to have a go at reining, which seems to be a really exciting discipline. With the help of my trainer, I'm starting spins and sliding stops, but unfortunately, I'm having trouble with my saddle. It was fitted for him but tends to slip back – is there anything that I can do to prevent this?

A Check your saddle fit again as, if your horse has become fitter or lost weight, your saddle may need adjusting. Using a Western breastcollar and/or a saddle pad with an underside grip layer may help. You can choose from a plain breastcollar or a more ornate design with silver inlays and embossed leather for shows.

To confuse matters, a Western breastcollar resembles an English breastplate more than it does an English breastcollar. When fitting it, allow a hand's width between the breastcollar and the chest and adjust it so the chest straps do not restrict the movement of the horse's shoulders.

5

CONTENTS

TRAINING AIDS

PROS AND CONS

There is a huge array of training aids on the market and a huge amount of controversy over their use. But as long as you accept that there is no such thing as a magic wand that will suddenly turn an uneducated or badly ridden horse into one who works beautifully on the bit, and that quick fixes usually become just as quickly undone, the right equipment, used in the right way, can be very valuable.

Some people are scathing about training aids and label them as gadgets. However, if you ask them if they use, say, side reins when lungeing a horse, they will inevitably say that these don't count because they are standard equipment.

In logical terms, anything that is used to help with a horse's training is a training aid, from a simple neckstrap to the latest piece of lungeing equipment. Just because something has been around for a long time, it doesn't mean it is a good idea: draw reins (see pages 114–15) are proof of that.

Similarly, there are plenty of new ideas that are both useful and humane and others that are illogical or an example of clever marketing. Bear in mind that a training aid should be just that – an aid to training.

Training aids do not have to be complicated, as the simple neckstrap shown here proves.

WHY USE A TRAINING AID?

If the purpose of training a horse is to enable him to carry himself and his rider comfortably and in balance, a training aid should help him to do that by encouraging the development of correct musculature. That, by definition, takes time: it's easy to get a horse to arch his neck and tuck in his nose, but he won't be able to work from behind and be truly on the bit until he is correctly developed.

It's also important to remember that a horse can only work within the limits of his conformation, though some can pleasantly surprise you. For instance, a horse who is croup-high will find it harder to lighten his forehand than one who is 'born on the bit'.

Training aids can also be used under veterinary supervision to rehabilitate horses after injury. For example, a Chambon or a lungeing system such as the Pessoa or EquiAmi may be recommended after initial healing has taken place for horses who have suffered back or pelvis injuries.

Check the fit of your saddle before using a training aid.

GOLDEN RULES

Before using a training aid to try to solve a problem or make an improvement in your horse's way of going, check his soundness, the fit of your saddle and bridle and your riding.

If your horse is sticking his head in the air because of dental problems, badly fitting tack or a rider who tries to force his head into an outline, a training aid won't help.

Give your horse time to get used to anything new – and be prepared for a reaction.

If you are satisfied that everything is in order, keep ten golden rules in mind as you decide what equipment to use:

1. Introduce new equipment with care and fit it loosely. This gives the horse a chance to get used to its action and to anything that feels different from his ordinary tack, such as poll pressure, or straps fitting round his hindquarters.

2. Only work him for short periods to start with – five minutes on each rein may be plenty at first. When you are asking him to adopt a different posture, he will use muscles that may not have been worked before and you don't want him to become stiff or uncomfortable.

3. Unless you are following a regime set out by your vet, or by a qualified practitioner working under veterinary supervision, don't use a training aid every day. Alternate work days with those when he is hacked on a loose rein, turned out to graze, or both.

4. For safety reasons, don't use equipment that is designed purely for lungeing, such as a Chambon or side reins, for riding. Side reins are standard when a rider is being given a lunge lesson, but the big difference is that the trainer, not the rider, controls the horse.

5. If you haven't used your chosen equipment before, find out as much about it as you can. Ideally, get someone who uses it successfully to work with you.

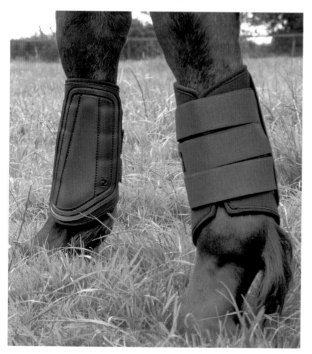

6. There is no such thing as a miracle training aid, just as there is no such thing as a miracle bit! To work correctly, a horse needs to build up his muscles correctly, and that takes time.

7. If you are using a training aid that attaches to the bit, only use it with a simple snaffle. Never use a bit that has a curb action or applies poll pressure, or you risk turning persuasion into force.

8. Unless you are working under veterinary supervision, warm up a horse without the training aid fitted. This allows his muscles to loosen before they are asked to take a particular posture.

9. Because he is working in an unfamiliar way, it's a good idea to fit protective boots in case he injures himself. In most cases, a simple pair of brushing boots is enough.

10. While some training aids may be suitable for adults to use on children's ponies, children should not be allowed to use them unsupervised. Some equipment, such as the Market Harborough, is suitable for children to use as long as they are supervised by a knowledgeable adult.

HEAD STARTS

Headcollars, lungeing cavessons and other standard equipment associated with leading and lungeing are often bought and used with little thought. But think about what you use and why you use it, and you could be surprised at how a small buy makes an enormous difference.

Headcollars range from top-quality made-to-measure leather models designed for smartness and safety when travelling and competing to budget-priced nylon webbing designs. Both should be fitted so that they neither rub the facial bones nor twist round and rub against the wearer's eye.

Unless your horse's facial proportions conveniently match those of an off-the-peg headcollar, spend a bit extra on a design that is adjustable at the nose as well as at the side of the face. Headcollars with a T-shaped section linking the noseband and cheekpieces tend to stay more stable – the Thorowgood design shown here enables you to remove and replace the T-section when grooming or clipping the face.

Thorowgood's headcollar enables you to groom or clip the horse's head while keeping hold of him.

MATERIAL COSTS

Nylon headcollars are strong and fine for everyday use, but should never be left on in the field or when a horse is unattended. If the horse gets it caught up on something in the field or stable, he could be badly injured or even break his neck.

If you need to leave a headcollar on your horse in the field – and it really is best avoided, as, apart from the risks outlined above, it makes a thief's job easier – use one with a breakaway ring or section.

Always try to use leather headcollars when travelling a horse, as these are strong enough to restrain him but will break in the case of an accident. 'Field safe' headcollars are not safe for travelling, as they will come undone too soon and could leave you with a horse trying to turn round in the horsebox or trailer.

You can buy breakaway devices to fit between the headcollar rope and the tying-up ring, but again, these may release too early.

Standard halters are simple designs made from webbing and rope, and are intended purely for leading. Unlike training halters (see page 100) they are not designed to slip and release as the horse responds to pressure and, unless they are knotted

The clip-out T-shaped section on this Thorowgood headcollar means you can groom or clip the horse's face safely, while staying in control.

at the jaw, will pull tight and remain so. They should not be used for tying-up.

Traditionally, some native pony breeds are shown in white webbing halters in the UK. From the point of view of safety, this can't be recommended and you shouldn't be penalized for using a proper headcollar or, if your pony is old enough to be bitted, a bridle.

If you want to lunge your horse without the lunge rein having a direct action on the bit, or to have a little more control than a standard headcollar affords, a well-made lungeing cavesson may be the answer. The noseband must be substantial enough to remain in place and have sufficient padding to prevent the three lunge rein rings from causing pressure points on the nose.

The standard lunge cavesson fastens above the bit and can be made from leather (desirable but expensive) or webbing. Some trainers use a Wels cavesson, which fastens below the bit, to give extra control.

One school of thought believes that lunge cavessons discourage the horse from going forward because of the psychological effect of the lunge rein being fastened at the front of the face – a similar theory to that behind the Australian cheeker noseband (see page 69) However, that view seems only to be held by the minority.

Most cavessons are fitted with three rings, and it's up to you whether you attach the lunge rein to the central one or to the appropriate side-ring. In general, the central ring works well because it means the cavesson is less likely to be pulled slightly to one side and you don't have to change the position of the lunge rein when you change the rein.

White rope halter.

Tail bandage between rope and tying-up ring.

'If I have a young horse who pulls back when he is tied up, I'll use a tail bandage as a loop between the rope and the tying-up ring instead of a piece of string. Because it's stretchy, it will give – so the horse has less to fight – but will break if the horse panics.'
Pippa Funnell, international event rider

LEAD TIMES

If you're showing a horse in-hand and leading him from the left side, there is a risk that his mouth will become desensitized or 'one-sided', especially if he is onward bound or excitable to start with and you struggle for control. To avoid this, use a coupling that fastens to the noseband and to both rings of a snaffle bit (see picture, page 79), thus keeping any pressure central and divided between the nose – a control point he is used to – and the mouth.

For everyday use, lead ropes made from soft rope or cotton webbing are fine, though check that when you tie the latter in a quick-release knot, it actually does release quickly – some materials stick, which won't help in an emergency. Clips must be of good quality and must be checked regularly to make sure their action isn't impeded by dirt; really cheap ropes often have poor-quality metal clips that are more likely to give way.

The ultimate in luxury lead ropes have leather at the end near the clip and leather sewn over the end nearest the rider's hand. These are expensive, but should last a long time as wear and tear on the rope is minimized.

Clips must be checked, cleaned and oiled if necessary.

A hand-stitched show lead rein with brass fittings.

A good-quality leadrope.

The ultimate all-in-one

The Rambo Micklem Multibridle is a very long name for a very clever idea. Designed by Irish international trainer William Micklem FBHS, it is a bridle, lunge cavesson and bitless bridle all in one and gives priority to the horse's comfort.

When fitted correctly, there is no pressure on the facial bones, poll or cheek tissues. There are also clips which hold the bit rings to the side-rings on the noseband, which reduces tongue pressure and keeps the bit at the correct height in the mouth – making it a particularly good choice for horses with difficult-to-solve tongue evasions and for young horses.

The Multibridle has a reinforced, shaped noseband with a central ring to which the lunge rein is attached. It fastens below the bit and works in a similar way to a Wels lunge cavesson, giving more control than an ordinary one. The other advantage of this design is that it is shaped to fit the face, so there is no risk of it slipping to one side.

Rambo Micklem Multibridle.

'When you first introduce a foal to being led from a headcollar rope, use a plain rope without a clip and slip it through the back of the headcollar. If a foal gets away from you on a clip rope, it could tangle round his legs and end in a fatal accident.'
Sue Rawding, UK breeder of sports and show horses

UNDER PRESSURE

Thanks to trainers such as Monty Roberts and Richard Maxwell, we have become much more aware of how teaching a horse to be responsive and obedient on the ground not only makes our relationship with him safer and more pleasant, but translates through to ridden work.

Groundwork techniques rely on teaching a horse to respond to pressure. This does not mean putting him under stress, but using it as a fair way of communicating with him. It must never become punishment or force.

Basic groundwork equipment includes rope halters marketed under different names. Some work by tightening on the nose and perhaps the poll when the horse resists, then automatically releasing the instant he responds.

Others do not self-adjust, but have knots at the side of the nose that may apply a little extra pressure to reinforce stopping, turning and backing-up instructions. There are also designs that have metal plates at the poll, but before using one, consider the consequences of such pressure being imposed on the delicate poll area.

Most trainers recommend that they be used with long ropes, either 4m (12ft) or 7m (20ft) depending on how much distance you want to put between you and the horse. Yachting rope is a favourite material, because it is strong, smooth to handle and slides when required without catching on itself.

Some ropes have a leather flap on the end to allow more definite signals, rather like Western-style riders' romal reins.

Knots at the side apply a little extra pressure.

Parelli enthusiasts place great emphasis on groundwork using their recommended halters and ropes.

'Whenever I get a new horse, I start by doing 80 per cent groundwork and 20 per cent ridden. Over two to three months, I reverse that to 80 per cent ridden and 20 per cent groundwork, but groundwork definitely becomes part of the whole schooling process forever.'
Richard Maxwell, trainer and expert on horse behaviour

THE DUALLY

The Dually headcollar, designed by Monty Roberts, gets its name from his old horse and because originally it could be used two ways: either as a standard headcollar or as a training aid. In fact, it has a third function, as it can also be used for riding as a form of sidepull bridle.

It should be fitted so that it is snug but not tight and so that the nose rope passes over the bridge of the nose without impinging on the soft area. When used for schooling, the lead rope or line clips to one or other of the side-rings, depending on which side you are working from.

It works by staying loose when the horse follows the handler appropriately and tightening when he resists or ignores. Monty stresses that the horse must be taught to understand its action and that users should practise using it on a large number of problem-free horses before attempting to correct a problem.

If you need to tie up a horse using a Dually, clip the rope to the centre back ring of the standard headcollar part. Never tie him up using the side-rings and never leave him alone or turn him out wearing a Dually, as the side-rings could get caught up on something.

While some headcollars have deliberate breakaway sections so that they come apart if they do get caught up, the Dually is a schooling device. If a breakaway were incorporated, it would not be suitable for use on strong or reactive horses as it would give way when you least wanted it to.

Whatever design of pressure headcollar or halter you choose, you need to teach your horse to respond to its action – don't expect to put it on and have an instantly obedient horse. Apply just as much pressure as you need via the lead rope or lunge line to get the desired reaction and as soon as the horse moves in the desired way, release the pressure.

Use a lead rope or training rope that is long enough to enable you to keep sufficient distance between you and the horse. It is sensible to wear a hard hat and gloves whenever you are training, for groundwork as well as ridden.

Your horse must be taught to understand the action of a headcollar such as the Dually.

Safety first
Never tie up or travel a horse in any form of pressure halter or headcollar. If he runs or pulls back and meets prolonged resistance, he could be badly hurt. Pressure equipment should never be used on foals and should always be used with thought and respect.

LUNGE AND SIDE REINS

Side reins are often regarded as standard equipment when lungeing a horse, but they are still classed as a training aid and there is a lot to think about in terms of design and adjustment, what you want to achieve from their use and even whether they are appropriate.

The purpose of side reins is to introduce the idea of a light contact on the bit and to help the horse realize that if he pushes against them, he will meet pressure, and if he holds himself in an appropriate way, he will be comfortable and not restricted. Because the appropriate carriage depends on his stage of training, it's important to get the choice and fitting correct.

The first decision is whether to use plain leather or webbing side reins, or ones with an elastic or rubber insert incorporated. Some trainers are adamant that one is always better than the other, but it's better to be open-minded and experiment, as horses often react to one kind better than the other.

As a starting point, try designs with elastic inserts. The logic behind this is that we aim to ride with an elastic contact, so why not start with one?

Elastic inserts allow some give.

Although it's logical to use elastic side reins to start with, some trainers believe that these encourage horses to lean on the bit. If this happens, use lots of transitions on the lunge and encourage the horse to work from behind by pointing the lunge whip behind the girth line. If the problem persists try using plain reins.

However, a horse who goes behind the bit and is reluctant to work into a contact will often be encouraged to do so by the use of elastic side reins.

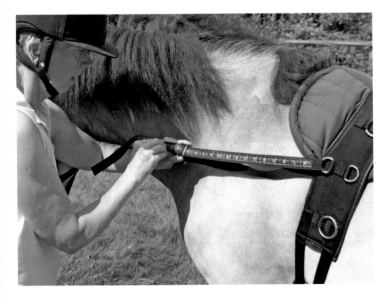

Side reins with markers for equal adjustment.

Whatever you decide on, choose side reins that allow you to adjust them to an equal length without guessing. Plain reins with slide adjustments aren't accurate enough: they should have markers, or buckles and holes.

First-timers

Side reins are usually introduced as part of the backing process. Teach the horse to walk, trot and halt before attempting to use them, then, when he is lungeing happily on a large circle, add a loose side rein on the outside rein – so, if you are starting on the left rein, you will fit the right side rein.

Attach it to the roller ring nearest in height to the point of the shoulder and to the outside cavesson side-ring. It should be loose enough for the horse to be aware of it, but not feel restricted.

When he is lungeing happily on the left rein, stop, change the side-rein to the left-hand side and repeat. Most horses are not at all worried by this and you can then fit both side reins.

Assuming that your horse is used to wearing a mild snaffle and to being led from it with a coupling, you can then fasten the side reins to the bit rings. Start by using just the outside side rein and when he lunges calmly on both reins in this way, fit both.

The side reins should be loose, but not so loose that as he moves, they flap around and jiggle the bit in his mouth. Over the space of a few days, shorten the side reins gradually so that you reach the stage where there is a light contact when the horse's nose is just in front of the vertical.

Introduce side reins by attaching them to the cavesson.

You can then move on to attaching them to the bit.

Lunge reins

Choose a lunge rein that is easy to handle. Some nylon designs are so lightweight they flap around and are unpleasant to hold even though you are (or should be) wearing gloves. The best design is, inevitably, the most expensive – soft but strong cotton webbing that is just heavy enough to hang nicely, with a swivel clip or strap and buckle at the end (below).

Making adjustments

Once a horse is established on the lunge, you may need to alter the height and length of the side reins to help overcome problems, or to use a different design.

If your horse leans on the bit and uses side reins to hold himself up, move them down to a lower ring and make sure that they are not too tight – adjusting them by even a hole can make a big difference.

For the opposite problem, that of the horse who tries to evade the side reins by raising his head and going in a hollow outline, positioning them slightly higher may help. It is sometimes recommended that crossing the side reins at the withers (below) and fastening the left one to the right side of the roller and vice versa will help with a horse who has an unsteady head carriage, but be careful the side reins are not too short.

Running side reins, sometimes called Vienna reins, are used on occasion by show producers and dressage trainers, especially when loose schooling. The mildest way of fitting them is to pass each one through a bit ring and to rings on the roller on the same side, but at different heights.

The advantage of this fitting is that it allows the horse more freedom to flex to the side, as the reins move through the bit rings. They can also be fastened to the roller at his belly, passed through the bit rings and then to the roller side-rings: this mimics the action of draw reins (see page 114) but doesn't rely on a rider's quick reactions to release them when a horse who comes above the bit lowers his head and neck.

Adjust the height of the side reins to suit your horse's way of going.

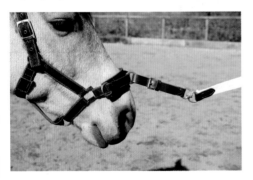

TIP

If you arrive at a show and need to lunge your horse to settle him, and have forgotten your side reins, you can improvise a pair using your ordinary reins. Unfasten them at the centre buckle, then wrap each half around the girth straps at an appropriate length and height.

'We use Vienna reins to encourage young horses to work from behind and build up the correct musculature over their backs and top line. We don't lunge very young horses because it puts too much strain on their joints, but we might use these on two-year-olds by trotting them down the long side of the school.'
Darren Blanchard, UK sports horse breeder and producer

Roller or saddle?

As it's perfectly possible to lunge a horse who is wearing a saddle, and fasten side reins and other training aids to the girth, buying a roller might seem an unnecessary expense. However, if you're backing a young horse, it's a much easier way to introduce the idea of something being fastened round his belly and he is less likely to take fright.

Leather rollers are covetable but expensive and there are plenty of lightweight synthetic rollers available. Perhaps the most practical of all are those that fasten on to an ordinary girth, allowing you to use them on horses and ponies of different sizes.

Use an appropriate pad or specially made roller pad underneath to help keep your horse comfortable and avoid pressure just behind his withers.

If you want to lunge an experienced horse using his saddle, either remove the stirrups and leathers altogether or secure them so they don't flap around and bang his sides. You can do this either by wrapping the stirrup leather round the iron, passing the end through the loop and then through the keeper on the saddle flap (see picture below), or by using a spare stirrup leather to fasten them under his belly.

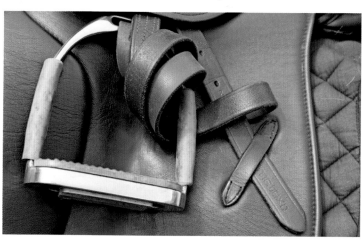

LONG-REINING

Long-reining, or long-lining, was a traditional part of backing and educating horses. It went out of fashion for a time but is now enjoying renewed popularity.

At its simplest, it can be used to teach a horse to go forward, stop and steer without him having to adjust his balance for a rider's weight, so when ridden work starts, he is halfway to understanding what's wanted. At another level, it can be used to teach advanced movements and airs above the ground, as at the Spanish Riding School of Vienna.

Lunge reins can be used as long reins, but it's important to choose ones that are comfortable to hold and that you can lengthen and shorten easily. If you haven't long-reined a horse before, it's a good idea to practise with one who knows what it's about and if necessary, to fasten the long reins to the side-rings of a lunge cavesson before attaching them to the bit.

Experienced riders and drivers who long-rein frequently often prefer to use leather driving reins or ropes because they feel they give more sensitive communication with the horse's mouth. The latter are sometimes called plough lines, as they were used when working horses in the fields.

When long-reining, you are obviously much further away from the horse's head than when riding, so you need to think about where you want the horse to go and what you want him to do in plenty of time. This applies particularly when long-reining on a straight line, sometimes referred to as driving, even when the horse is being trained for riding.

The reins along the side of the horse's body can also mimic the action of the rider's leg, so you can ask him to turn by opening the inside rein slightly and bringing the outside rein against his side as you would your outside leg.

SAFETY FIRST

Introduce long reins in a safe environment, with someone at the horse's head to reassure him. Move them along his neck and back so that he gets used to their presence, then slide them gently over his hindquarters and down his leg, making sure you stand far enough away that you can't get kicked. Some horses cow kick

(kick forwards) when they first feel the long reins above their hocks.

The next stage is to move the reins from one side to the other to reproduce changing the rein when long-reining on a circle. When the horse accepts all this calmly, you're ready to long-rein properly.

If he continues to resent the long reins round his quarters, a technique that sometimes works is to fasten a soft rope to the side-ring of a roller, pass it round his quarters and fasten it to the roller ring on the other side. Lead and lunge him as normal wearing this, again, keeping out of kicking range, and he should soon become desensitized.

When long-reining on a straight line, it's safer to stand slightly to one side rather than directly behind the horse. This also gives more control if he takes off and you're less likely to be towed behind him.

However, change your position regularly so that you're not always on the same side, and when you turn, move slightly to the direction in which you want him to go.

On a straight line, it's safer to stand slightly to one side of your horse.

Use a soft rope fastened to the roller with quick-release knots to accustom a horse to long reins if necessary.

FITTING OPTIONS

Many trainers like to fit long reins that pass straight from the bit to the hand, feeling that this gives the most sensitive communication. But if you're long-reining a horse on straight lines as part of his education, perhaps driving him down tracks or even very quiet roads, it's safer to pass them through stirrups or, if your roller has them fitted, through large rings level with the point of his shoulder.

If you use a saddle and stirrups, adjust the stirrups so that they are above the height of your horse's elbow and so can't bang against this area as he moves. You also need to link them via a stirrup leather fastened under his belly, or to fasten them to the girth, so they don't flap around.

If you pass the long reins through roller rings, make sure the rings are large enough to allow them to run freely. The advantage of keeping the reins at a fixed height is that if the horse whips round, it's easier to prevent the long reins dangling round his feet. The disadvantage is that you can't open the rein as easily. You need to weigh up the pros and cons.

You also have to decide whether to use loose side reins when long-reining. Their advantage is that they give extra control and prevent the horse putting his head to down to graze or throwing it up and down as a resistance; the disadvantage is that you may get a less definite communication because both the side reins and the long reins are fastened to the bit.

It really is a matter of looking at your horse, his stage of training, his attitude and what you're trying to achieve and experimenting to find the safest and most effective set-up.

'I prefer light, thin reins, because if they're too heavy, they can pull excessively on the mouth even before you take a contact. Usually they're identical, but if a horse is very heavy on one hand, I'll put an even lighter rein on this side to encourage me to take a lighter contact and the horse to step more into the other rein, straightening his body.'
Michele Thornton, former manager at the International League for the Protection of Horses

The Feeline approach

If you find working with two reins difficult, or simply want to try something designed to give a feel more similar to that achieved when riding, the Feeline could be the answer. Designed by international rider and trainer Claire Lilley, this literally turns two reins into one and makes working on a circle much easier.

It consists of a single long rein with sliding and static clips that attach to the bit and roller rings. This enables you to long-rein, or, as Claire terms it, 'double-lunge', your horse, holding the reins as if you are riding.

The principles are exactly the same: the inside rein asks the horse to flex slightly, and the outside rein controls the speed and the amount of bend. As when using ordinary long reins on a circle, start with the outside rein over his back, then when you are both confident, bring it behind and round the hindquarters, where it should rest above the hocks.

The Feeline is logically designed to be used as part of a three-stage programme that allows the horse's muscles to build up and strengthen correctly. The first stage uses a Chambon (see page 110); the second uses side reins and the third brings in the Feeline so that the horse puts his back end underneath him and lightens his forehand.

CHAMBON AND DE GOGUE

The Chambon and de Gogue, both supposedly named after the French cavalry officers who invented them, have always been the first choice in training equipment for many European trainers. As more international riders broadened their training horizons, they became accepted in the UK and the USA and the Chambon is now regarded as a classic training aid.

Used correctly, it encourages a horse to stretch over his topline and, just as important, use and strengthen his abdominal muscles. To lift his back, a horse first has to lift his abdominals. It must only be used for lungeing or loose schooling because if it is coupled with a direct rein, the horse will be given conflicting signals.

The de Gogue is similar to, and in some ways an extension of, the Chambon, and is designed to achieve the same aims. It can be used for lungeing or riding; in the right hands, it can be very useful but wouldn't, perhaps, be a first choice for riding unless you have really good hands and quick reactions.

FITTING AND USING THE CHAMBON

The Chambon has two parts: a poll pad with a small ring positioned at each end, which buckles to the bridle headpiece, and a second piece that fastens to the girth and splits into two cord or rolled leather straps ending in clips. The cords run through the rings on the poll pads and down the horse's face and clip to the bit rings.

It works through a combination of gentle pressure on the poll, via the padded headpiece, and on the mouth. As with all the best training aids, the horse rewards himself when he answers its action.

If he lifts his head too high, the Chambon asks him to lower it and as long as he is kept moving actively forward, but not chased or hurried, he will bring his hind legs underneath him and stretch down. Some horses seem to enjoy Chambon work and will stretch forward and down so that their nose is nearly on the ground – a bit like equine Pilates.

When introducing it, fasten the clips to the rings on the poll straps so that you introduce poll pressure on its own. When he accepts this, clip it to the bit rings. It should be loose to start with and gradually be adjusted so that it comes into action when the horse's head is too high.

If you're lucky enough to have a round pen, or can fence off part of an arena to make a smaller area, this is an ideal way to introduce a Chambon. If you're using part of your arena, try to arrange your barriers so you make an octagon-shape to work in – this way, the horse won't get trapped in a corner and is less likely to try to jump out.

As with most aids used for lungeing, the trot is the most effective pace in which to work a horse. Some trainers use the Chambon when cantering a horse, but this puts much heavier demands on him and should only be done by experienced trainers working mature, sound and established horses.

When introducing the Chambon, fasten the clips to the poll strap rings (inset) until the horse is used to poll pressure.

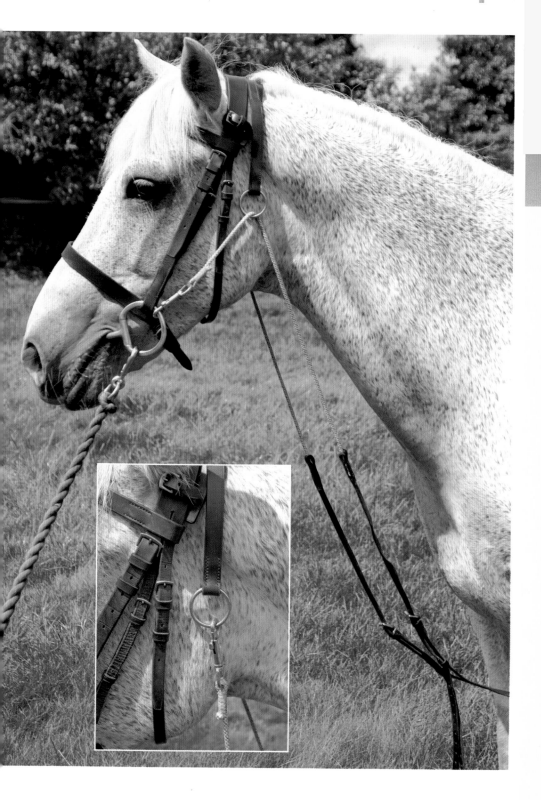

THE DE GOGUE

While the Chambon should only be used when lungeing and loose schooling, the de Gogue can also be used when riding. Many trainers who use it prefer to start by lungeing in a Chambon, then move on to riding in a de Gogue, as they feel the two complement each other.

The design of the de Gogue is similar in that it has the same poll strap with a ring at each end and also has a second part, which fastens at the girth and incorporates two cords or straps. The difference is that this time, the straps run through the bit rings rather than being fastened directly to them.

It can be used in two ways, usually called the independent and the direct fittings. Always introduce it via the independent fitting, which, as its name suggests, means it is independent of the rider's hands, and unless you are sure of your ability to remain balanced and ride with sympathetic hands whatever the horse does, stick to it!

Used in this way, the straps run through the bit rings and those on the poll strap, then go back to the main strap at the chest. This creates what is often described as 'a triangle of control', which allows enough freedom of the head and neck but comes into action via poll and bit pressure when the horse raises his head too high.

When he responds by lowering his head and neck, the pressure is immediately released. Start by lungeing or loose schooling so that he gets used to its action, then use it for riding with a direct rein attached to the snaffle rings.

Direct communication

The direct fitting is only used for riding and, in all honesty, 99 per cent of riders probably shouldn't employ it. Like draw reins (see pages 114–15), it relies on the rider being able to release the rein at a precise moment.

Again, the cords run through the bit and poll strap rings, but this time are attached to a rein going to the rider's hands. In theory, and unlike many training aids, it can be used for jumping as well as riding on the flat.

The de Gogue creates a triangle of control.

Safety first

In very skilled hands, the de Gogue can be effective in persuading horses who set their necks against the rider, which is an evasion many cobs use. But – and it is a big but – it must always be loose enough not to force the horse into an outline.

If you want to use a de Gogue, it's recommended that you try one such as the version shown here, the Barnsby FTS design.

This is made with interchangeable rope and elastic and you should certainly at least start with the elastic.

If you use it in the direct fitting, ride with a second rein going straight to the bit rings and hold the two as you would the reins on a double bridle. This means you can ride on the ordinary rein and only use the de Gogue rein when needed.

The Barnsby FTS de Gogue has a degree of elasticity, which many horses prefer.

'In the right hands – and they've got to be the right hands – a de Gogue can encourage a horse to make a good shape over a fence. If you haven't used one before, don't try it without getting help from someone who understands it.'
Tom Vance, show jumping trainer and former member of the Irish show jumping team

DRAW AND RUNNING REINS

As with all the tack and equipment included in this book, it is up to the individual to decide on the value or otherwise of draw and running reins. My personal opinion is that their drawbacks far outweigh their advantages, and that there are much better alternatives, but if you have a reason for using them, please be aware that they can cause more problems than they solve.

Although the terms are often interchanged, draw and running reins have different uses. Draw reins pass through the bit rings and fasten at the girth under the belly, whereas running reins fasten to the girth at the side.

The easiest way to remember the difference is that draw reins 'draw the head down'. In fact, they can exert a lot of leverage and the horse will nearly always overbend when they are used. Adherents say that overbending while draw reins are employed translates to a correct head carriage when they are removed, but that doesn't always follow.

Running reins exert less leverage and, while they ask the horse to bring in his head, they don't ask him to lower it. In one way, this means they are less severe, and some trainers will use them as a quick fix to keep a horse straight, but the danger is that they can also restrict his movement through the shoulder.

Horses nearly always overbend when ridden in draw reins.

'Running and draw reins must only be used by an experienced rider who can get a horse forward and in front of the leg. The rider must be capable of riding on the normal snaffle rein and only using the draw reins momentarily during a half halt. They should never be used by novice or inexperienced riders – and should only be used when retraining problem horses.'
Richard Davison, international dressage rider

Kinder alternatives

Why use draw or running reins when there are much kinder alternatives? The one that is most closely related to draw reins is the Barnsby FTS Soft Touch, which has a pulley at the girth and so should minimize the risk of a horse being fixed into an outline.

Running reins exert less leverage than draw reins.

Always use a direct rein as well as the draw rein.

DOUBLE UP

If you must use draw or running reins, always attach a pair of ordinary reins to the bit rings and use these as the dominant rein. Never use draw or running reins on their own, because you'll continually pull in your horse's head to an unacceptable angle, will cause him physical and psychological distress and will actually have very little control.

Hold them as you would the reins of a double bridle or pelham, with the ordinary, direct rein on the outside of the little fingers and the other rein between the little fingers and third fingers. Ask with the direct rein first, then, if necessary, with the second one.

The moment the horse responds to its action, release it. It must literally be split-second timing, or you are not rewarding his reaction and, therefore, reinforcing the fact that he has responded correctly.

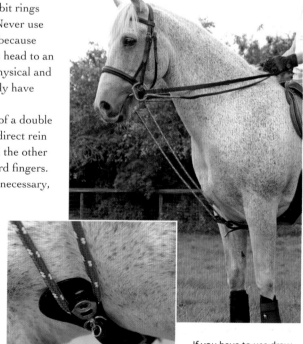

If you have to use draw reins, the Barnsby FTS Soft Touch is less restrictive.

GIVE AND TAKE

Many of the best training aids incorporate elastic rope that has a small amount of 'give'. This means that when the horse resists, usually by raising his head too high, he gets plenty of warning before it comes fully into action.

It's the difference between asking a polite question and saying, 'You will do this'. Ask yourself which approach you would prefer and it's easy to see why a bit of give is better than a lot of take.

ELASTIC SCHOOLING REIN

The simplest idea is the elastic schooling rein or bungee rein. This is a long elastic rope with clips at each end that goes over the poll, through the bit rings and clips to the girth, either under the belly or at the sides.

Because it has a reasonable amount of 'give', most horses accept it calmly. Its other big advantage is that it is pretty idiot-proof: although its length needs to be adjusted to suit each individual horse, it is easy to see when it is short enough to come into play at the correct time, and the elasticity gives extra leeway.

The horse rewards himself; when he raises his head too high, it employs gentle pressure on the poll and through the bit rings, but as soon as he lowers his head, the pressure is released.

Some horses will always resist even gentle poll pressure. In this situation, the first step is to make sure that there are no physical or psychological problems; the first can be identified by your vet and the second may be due to previous incorrect riding or use of training aids.

Lungie Bungie

If equipment that utilizes poll pressure continues to be unsuitable for such a horse, the Lungie Bungie, developed by Australian event rider Clayton Fredericks, could be the answer. It can be used for riding or lungeing and comprises a short strap with a central ring and an elastic rope that passes through the ring and fastens to the saddle or roller.

Its action is similar to side reins, but it doesn't limit the horse's lateral flexion, which is why it is safe to use when riding, whereas side reins are too restrictive. Many trainers find it useful for improving horses' canter, as it is said to help them find their balance without giving them something to lean on.

The elastic schooling rein has a more definite action when attached to the girth between the front legs, but is infinitely preferable to draw reins.

The Lungie Bungie can be used for lungeing or riding.

The Harbridge acts directly on the bit.

The EquiAmi isn't restrictive and the horse is less likely to pull or lean.

Harbridge

The Harbridge is another idea that doesn't employ poll pressure. It works via two elasticated straps that clip to the snaffle rings. Some trainers believe it's no more than the equivalent of clipping side reins from the girth through the front legs to the bit, but others report good results on horses who throw up their heads.

BOTTOMS UNDER!

A horse can't work truly on the bit until he has the muscles that enable him to do so. The Pessoa and the EquiAmi lungeing systems are designed to encourage him to work from behind into a round, but not overbent, outline and have won many devotees, including experts in rehabilitation work.

Although they look complicated, they are easy to fit and use. The EquiAmi is perhaps more logical, as it places the horse inside a 'self-centring loop', which mimics the connection formed between the rider's arms, shoulders, hands and reins. As it isn't fixed, the horse isn't restricted and is less likely to resist or lean.

Reminder

Any training aid used for lungeing can only be effective if the horse is lunged correctly. Letting him slop round, or, alternatively, making him rush, will be counterproductive. If you aren't sure about your lungeing skills, get help from a good trainer. Don't use any training aid when jumping unless it is specifically designed to be safe for this purpose.

TRAINING AIDS FOR RIDERS

Training aids don't necessarily need to affect the horse directly. There are lots of useful items that are, in effect, training aids for riders, and because they help the rider, they also help the horse.

The simplest one of all is the neckstrap, which can be either a spare stirrup leather buckled round the horse's neck, or the neckstrap of a martingale or breastplate. It not only provides a useful 'grab-handle' in emergency situations, but also can be used to reinforce downward transitions and half-halts and help you ensure you aren't relying on the reins too much as directional aids.

A neckstrap needs to be loose enough for you to be able to slip your fingers underneath it, without being so loose it falls down the horse's neck. This is where an English hunting breastplate has the advantage, because the straps that fasten it to the D-rings of the saddle keep it in place.

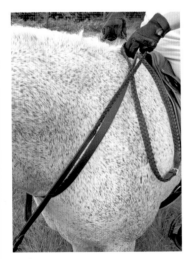

Neckstrap.

A breastplate can double up as a neckstrap.

Balance or bucking strap.

Symmetry leg-training straps.

If your horse rushes, or falls on to his forehand when making a downward transition, sit upright, think about allowing your upper body to stretch upwards and use your abdominal muscles to keep you centred. At the same time, slide your fingers under the neckstrap and give a short pull back, without pulling on the reins. The same technique will also help you introduce or reinforce a half-halt.

When you're riding school figures, it can also be a salutary lesson to hold the neckstrap as well as the reins. This makes you concentrate on looking where you are going, using your weight and leg aids, and keeping your hands as a pair as you turn.

A neckstrap gives security to novice riders, both physically and psychologically, and can help save the horse's mouth from the effects of wobbly hands. It also reminds inexperienced, and experienced, riders that to keep the hands still, particularly in rising trot, means allowing the elbow joint to open and close.

Some riders don't like using a neckstrap because they feel it encourages them to tip forward. In this case, a balance strap (also called a bucking strap) can be the answer. This is simply a rolled leather strap that clips to the D-rings of the saddle; slipping a finger underneath while you keep hold of the reins makes it easier to stay central.

It is often recommended for riders of big-moving Warmbloods and, like the neckstrap, is permitted under international dressage rules. For some reason, many riders seem to think that a neckstrap doesn't fit in with their image but that a balance strap is socially acceptable.

There is also an answer to the problem of wobbly legs. Many of us are so anxious to keep a correct leg position that we tend to push our lower legs too far back, particularly when doing lateral work. Symmetry leg-training straps are a simple but effective idea for adult riders that allow you to adopt a correct position until it becomes automatic.

REINS TO THE RESCUE

Many riders run into control problems when jumping, and in other potentially exciting situations, such as cantering their horse in company. What often happens is that the horse gradually pulls the reins through the rider's hands, putting him or her off balance and setting up a tug of war.

Riding technique obviously has a lot to do with it, in particular making sure that your lower leg is secure and you can use your abdominal muscles to help you stay centred. There is also a technique favoured by jockeys called 'bridging the reins', where you link them at the withers as shown (below) and which means that the horse is pulling against himself rather than against you.

This doesn't give enough handling flexibility for jumping a course of fences with frequent changes of direction, but it has provided the basis of a clever piece of equipment called the Mailer bridging rein. Invented by UK show jumping trainer Carol Mailer, it comprises a pair of reins with scallop-shaped grips allowing a bridging loop to link left and right.

The idea is that you fasten the bridging loop slightly further back from where you would normally hold the reins; you can then hold them in the normal position, but have a bridging position the moment the horse tries to pull forward or yank down. Because it creates less bulk than bridging a pair of ordinary reins, it's comfortable to use and is suitable for children as well as adults.

TIP

The Mailer bridging rein is also useful when schooling horses that don't pull. Because it encourages you to ride with your hands as a pair, it minimizes the risk of carrying one hand higher than the other and/or using too much inside rein and not enough outside rein. Using it for this purpose can be a salutary lesson no matter how experienced you are – you might be surprised how much easier it is to keep your horse straight.

'The Mailer bridging rein is simple and non-restrictive. It encourages the rider to hold the reins at the correct length and is also sympathetic to the horse's mouth, as the rider doesn't have to be strong to keep the correct feel.'
John Bowen, leading UK trainer

FLEXIBLE FRIENDS

While we all try to ride with the proverbial elastic contact, it's sometimes easier said than done. Reins with elastic inserts, or elastic 'buffers' that restrict the amount of contact you can take without reducing control, can be a reminder of what you should be feeling through the reins.

Another idea, which often appeals to young riders, is to use reins which have multi-coloured rubber grips. Rather than having to keep telling their pupils to shorten their reins, instructors can remind them to keep their hands within a certain colour section.

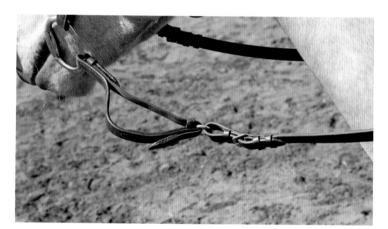

Elastic inserts can give a reminder of what you should be feeling through the reins.

Reins with multi-coloured grips are a useful teaching aid.

TTEAM WORK

Canadian trainer Linda Tellington-Jones was one of the first trainers using non-traditional methods to make a wide-ranging impact on the horse world. She developed the Tellington Touch Equine Awareness Method (TTEAM), graduating from massage and the Feldenkrais method – which focuses on whole body awareness – to her own system.

As part of the TTEAM approach, practitioners use a specific lead line and a long, stiff white dressage stick to give clear signals. The lead line has a chain or rope section at the clip end and if you are leading from the left, passes through the left side-ring, across the headcollar noseband and out through the lower right side-ring. It then clips to the upper right side-ring.

When horses are anxious, stiff or lazy, it can sometimes seem as if the two halves of their body are not connected: that the front end doesn't know what the back end is doing. Linda Tellington-Jones has devised the body wrap and the body rope to help; both work on the same principle, but the wrap gives a less definite feel and may be the best one to try first.

You can buy a body wrap, or make one from two elastic bandages (tail bandages are ideal) fastened round the horse's body. Wrap and knot the first bandage round the horse's neck, then pull it back as you attach the second so that it rests just behind the withers.

The second bandage fits round the hindquarters and rests just below the point of the buttocks, lying snugly enough not to slide down the horse's hind legs as he moves. As always, introduce it in a safe environment and be aware that some horses might kick the first time they feel the wrap round their back end.

The body rope follows the same pattern and is made from a single length of soft rope tied in a figure of eight round the horse's body. It should be twisted at the withers and tied using a quick-release knot. The knot must be sited so that the handler is able to release it easily.

RIDING WITH A WRAP

TTEAM practitioners use modified wraps and ropes fastened round the hindquarters and fastened to the girth straps when riding, to solve specific problems. Wraps are said to help horses who shy, are frightened of things behind them, or who drop their backs. Ropes are suggested for those who don't use their hindquarters well, or who drag their toes or kick.

However, if your horse demonstrates one of the above problems, it is vital that you get him checked by a specialist equine vet to find out if there are physical problems that need treating.

It may well be that using a body wrap or rope could help as part of a rehabilitation process, but if, for instance, a horse drags his toe because he has a suspensory ligament problem, the first step must be to get a proper diagnosis and treatment.

Remember that buying the right equipment will only give you the right results if you know how to use it correctly. When it is part of a philosophy such as this, you need to look at the big picture; see the Useful Contacts section (page 183) for details of TTEAM work.

WHIPS AND SPURS

To people who aren't horsey, and even to some who are, whips and spurs have connotations of cruelty. While it's true they can be abused, they can also be useful and humane ways of fine-tuning your communication.

Should you ever smack a horse? Views on this are as fierce as those on smacking children. While most people would find hitting a horse to cause pain not acceptable, a smart tap that doesn't hurt but produces an instant 'go forward' response is kinder, in the long run, than continually nagging at a horse whose sides have been dulled by constant kicking.

ON THE LUNGE

When lungeing a horse, a long whip, usually a lungeing whip, though some people prefer a shorter 'dealer' whip, helps the trainer keep him forward and can also help prevent him falling in. It should be a comfortable weight and feel balanced – you should be able to let it rise and fall without struggling to keep it in position.

The whip can be used as a pointer, or to give little flicks towards the horse, but never to hit him. Cracking it can also provide encouragement to a horse who doesn't understand how to go forward, as long as you don't say 'Go' with the whip and 'Stop' by jerking on the lunge line.

Handling a lungeing whip takes practice and you need to practise without a horse. You might get some funny looks, but it will be worth it in the end.

'If it's used correctly, a whip is simply another aid. It should not be something for the horse to be frightened of.'
Jennie Loriston-Clarke, international dressage rider and trainer

IN THE SADDLE

Schooling whips, used to reinforce the leg aid or to ask the horse to move a specific hind leg, range from about 110cm (43in) to almost fishing-rod length. They are designed to allow you to touch or flick the horse by moving your wrist and forearm, without taking a hand off the rein, so it's important not to pull back.

Some horses are nervous of them, either because they have been hit with one or because they can see the end moving as if something is chasing them. It's possible to desensitize a horse from the ground by stroking him with a schooling whip on both sides; you can then gradually raise and lower it from side to side over the withers to mimic the rider changing it from one side to the other.

More rigid designs are better than ones that bend and bounce, as they are less likely to worry the horse when he catches sight of them. Some horses happily accept a schooling whip carried in the rider's right hand, but are nervous if it is carried in the left. This is often because they are used to being handled and tacked up from the left: if you spend time desensitizing such a horse by stroking him with a schooling whip, starting at the shoulder and gradually moving back, he will usually learn to accept it.

Safety first
Never hit a horse with a schooling whip. It is an extra signal, not a punishment, and can potentially inflict a lot of pain and damage. He will also remember it – as the old saying goes: Lose your temper and you lose your horse.

A schooling whip is used without taking the hand off the rein.

Short options

Short whips, traditionally and unfortunately known as cutting whips, are more practical for riding out and jumping. They should not be used to punish, but to reinforce or encourage, for instance, tapping a horse on the shoulder may encourage him to step forward and holding a short whip down the shoulder will encourage a horse not to fall out on that side, both on the flat and when jumping.

To use a short whip behind the girth, you need to take your hand off the rein to avoid pulling back on the horse's mouth. To change a short or schooling whip from one hand to the other, follow the picture sequence – it's much safer and neater than pulling the whip through your hand.

Hand loops are often fitted to short whips, especially those meant for children. Using these is not recommended, as there have been cases of riders falling and breaking their wrists – it's better to cut off the loop in case the user forgets about this.

Show jumpers often use extra-short whips, because these are easier to hold or tap down the horse's shoulder to encourage him to keep straight.

Hand loops are dangerous if they get caught up or the rider falls.

To change a whip from one hand to the other safely, follow this sequence. Keep your movements quiet – don't wave the whip around. Some horses may be startled when the rider changes a whip from one hand to the other, whatever method is used, so if you're riding one you don't know – perhaps when trying a prospective purchase – be careful.

1 In this case, the whip is held in the left hand and will be transferred to the right.
2 Hold the reins in the left hand and place the right hand below the left.
3 Tilt the whip up and over the horse's neck.
4 When it is in its new position, take up the reins in both hands again.

Wip wops work

The wip wop, or over and under, is an alternative aid to encourage a horse to go forward. This short length of rope follows the same principle as Western romal reins and is flipped from side to side, over the horse's neck and behind the rider's leg.

Take the hand holding the wip wop off the reins before using this aid, or you could accidentally catch the horse in the mouth. When introducing it, it's also a good idea to slip the fingers of your other hand under a neckstrap, as some horses will be so surprised by it that they leap forward – and as you're looking for any sort of forward impetus, you don't want to catch him in the mouth.

Colour and comfort

Some riders and trainers think that the colour of a whip affects the horse's reaction to it. In particular, some practitioners of the Tellington Touch Equine Awareness Method believe that a white whip, or wand, as they term it, is more effective for getting a horse's attention.

You can also choose a whip that will put some colour and bling into your life. If you're one of many who like to think pink, you'll find whips to suit, and there are also plenty of styles featuring glitter, diamante and fancy flaps.

It's also possible to combine bright looks with safety. Whips in fluorescent yellow aren't sufficient as a road safety measure when used alone, but can be added to other measures – and if you drop them, or they go missing on a yard, they're among the easiest to find.

Other ideas include whips with flashing lights on the top and designs incorporating small mirrors, supposed to help you see traffic approaching from behind without having to turn round in the saddle.

If you're going to be able to hold both your whip and your reins comfortably, you need to make sure that a whip handle is the right thickness and texture. Leather grips look stylish but can slide, which makes it more likely you'll drop the whip; rubber might not be as smart, but does help with grip.

Noise value

If you need to encourage a horse to go forward, choose a whip with a broad flap at the end that makes a slapping noise when tapped against the horse. Even better, tap it on the side of your boot or chaps.

If you ever visit a dealer's yard and notice a short length of rigid blue pipe, about the same diameter as a hosepipe, lying around, you've spotted a nagsman's secret weapon. These unconventional 'whips' aren't used to beat horses, but make a noise when tapped against the side or shoulder.

Hunting and showing whips

The traditional hunting whip has a bone handle designed to make opening gates easier, a thong and a lash. There are three treasonable offences in hunting circles: the first is to use a hunting whip without a thong and lash, the second is to hold it upside down – the handle should be nearest the ground – and the third is to call it a hunting crop.

> ## TIP
> Check competition rules for the type and length of whip allowed, as you may be eliminated for contravening them.

In the UK, it is correct for show hunter and show cob riders who wear a hunting cap and black jacket for championships and some afternoon and evening performances to carry a hunting whip.

For most show classes, a show cane, either plain bamboo or covered with leather, is correct. It should be held so that the same amount appears above and below the rider's hand. Side-saddle riders carry longer, slimmer canes, often with silver tops.

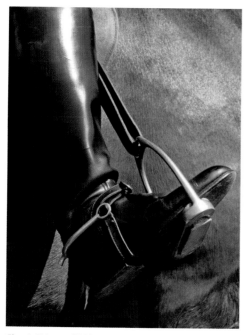

Classic Prince of Wales spurs at the correct height.

SPURS

The golden rule about spurs is that they should only be used by riders who are sufficiently balanced to apply them when they want to. They are designed to give finesse to the rider's aids, not to make them more severe.

English spurs range from the classic, blunt-ended Prince of Wales design in various lengths to spurs with rowels. Plain rowels are held by many trainers to be kinder than blunt spurs, because they move against the horse's side without digging in; however, sharp rowels can't be condoned.

Western competition spurs are works of art with ornate decoration on metalwork and straps. They nearly always have rowels and some would shock many English-style riders. However, some authorities say they originate in rodeo riding and were designed to give balance and grip on bulls with tough hides.

If you're thinking of using spurs for the first time, or need to introduce a young or sensitive horse to them, roller ball spurs can be useful. These have small, rotating plastic balls at the end, which brush against the horse's side but can't dig in.

Spur straps can be made from leather or nylon; nylon straps are fine for everyday use, but leather is much smarter for competition. They should be adjusted so that the spurs are at ankle height, not hanging down near the heel of your boot.

The 'bling' factor

Looking for a bit of bling? Apart from ornate Western spurs, you'll have a long way to go to beat one glamorous international show jumper, whose boyfriend was rumoured to have bought her a pair of spurs with inset diamonds for her birthday. However, there are gold-coloured spurs, spurs set with fake gemstones and spur straps incorporating diamante trim for riders so inclined.

QUESTIONS AND ANSWERS

Q My daughter's pony is very well behaved except when she gets on grass. She then puts her head down to eat, nearly pulling my daughter over her head. Is there anything I can do to give her more control?

A As ponies can be incredibly strong when it comes to food, you'll probably find that even a stronger rider would find it difficult to break this habit. The answer is to use a pair of grass or daisy reins.

You can buy grass reins or make your own from two lengths of thin, strong rope or baler twine. Fasten one end to the bit ring, then pass it up the side of the pony's face and thread it through the browband loop. Adjust it so it is long enough not to interfere with the pony's head movement while she is being ridden, but short enough to prevent her getting her head down, then tie it to the D-ring on the saddle.

Daisy reins are a similar idea, but attach to the bridle headpiece, run along the top of the pony's head and fasten to the saddle Ds. Some people prefer them because they don't have a connection to the bit, but their disadvantage is that they can pull the bridle back.

As horse sense is absolutely nothing compared to the cunning of many ponies, you should find that once the pony realizes she has been thwarted, she'll behave. Unfortunately, she'll also be quick to realize when the reins have been removed.

Q I need to lunge my horse for a few minutes at a show before I get on him, as he gets excited. Last time I tried to do this, using a lunge cavesson and side reins, he got away from me. Should I lunge him from the bit, instead – and if so, how do I attach the lunge rein?

A In an ideal world, it's better not to lunge a horse from the bit, as if you are using side reins or any other equipment you could be giving contradictory messages via the bit. In the real world, you can't endanger yourself or other riders and must be in control, so lungeing from the bit is the only sensible action.

There are two acceptable ways of doing this. One is to use a connecting strap between the bit rings and to attach the lunge rein to this; by using a connector, you won't be putting pressure on just one side of the mouth.

The other, which gives maximum control, is to fasten the lunge rein over the horse's head. If you are lungeing on the left rein, pass the rein through the left bit ring, over the horse's poll, down the right hand side of his face and clip it to the offside bit ring. When you change the rein, change the fastening so that it goes through the right bit ring, over the poll and fastens to the nearside bit ring.

Some riders simply clip the lunge rein to the inside bit ring, but this pulls the horse's head to the inside so you can't keep him straight and going forward. There is also a risk that the bit will pull through the horse's mouth.

If you haven't already done so, try taking your horse to some shows without competing him. Let him settle, then just ride him round the showground so he can get used to the sights and sounds and relax. Doing this a few times should help him to treat the whole experience more calmly.

Q I've been lungeing my horse on a Chambon, but he seems to dislike having the poll piece buckled to his bridle and tosses his head about when he starts working. Should I ignore it, or is there a problem I haven't spotted?

A Some Chambon designs have poll pieces with straight edges, which can catch the base of the ears and irritate the horse. You would probably find that he is happier with a curved poll piece, though these are harder to find.

6

PROTECTIVE BOOTS & BANDAGES

CONTENTS

BOOTS AND BANDAGES

Horses' legs are vulnerable and valuable and there are times when boots or bandages are essential. However, it's important to make sure they are well designed, suit the conformation of the horse's leg and are fit for a particular use.

Do you choose boots or bandages? Boots are often quicker and easier to use, but sometimes, correctly applied bandages are even better, so it's well worth honing your skills.

If you're a competitor, it's also important to read the rulebooks. For instance, leg protection is not allowed under international dressage rules, though it can be used when warming up: this means you need to allow time for a helper to remove boots or wraps before you enter the arena.

Boots and bandages are also prohibited in showing classes where the horse is not asked to jump, as the judge needs to assess the horse's conformation. They can be used in the jumping phase of working hunter classes in the UK, but are not used in equivalent classes in the USA.

Although veterinary bandaging is a subject on which you need specialist veterinary advice, there is a new generation of legwear that can help prevent common problems or provide comfort. Even the most traditional groom can benefit from new ideas.

Tails can also be vulnerable, and bandaging or using a tailguard will help prevent hair at the dock being rubbed and broken, which can occur if a horse leans back against a breeching bar or ramp to keep his balance.

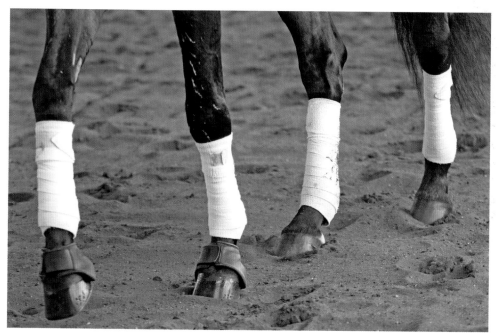

Some riders, especially dressage specialists, like to use bandages when schooling. Some designs incorporate a slightly padded section which goes next to the leg, then a stretch section made from thinner fabric. However, most vets advise that bandages should always be applied over separate padding to minimize the risk of pressure points on the leg, particularly over the tendons and ligaments.

PROTECTION GUIDELINES

There are some scenarios when leg protection is essential, though even then, there are caveats. For instance, as a general rule it's best to use boots or bandages when travelling a horse, but they should not be put on brood mares with foals at foot or the foals themselves.

Boots are a standard requirement when lungeing, as the horse is being asked to work on a relatively small circle and may not keep his balance consistently. They should also be fitted to young or unschooled animals, as there is more risk of them knocking themselves or overreaching.

Horses who move badly because of their conformation should also wear boots for protection. The most common defects that occur are brushing, where the horse knocks one limb against its partner on the opposite side, and overreaching, where he strikes the heel of one of his front feet with the toe of a hind one.

A horse who stumbles or trips, either because he is weak or because he is on the forehand, needs protection in the knee area when ridden on the roads. However, he should be checked out by your vet, as some conditions predispose a horse to stumbling, and treatment and perhaps a change in shoeing may be needed.

Veterinary advice should also be sought about the best way of protecting a horse who has previously suffered damage to a tendon or ligament.

Protective boots are essential when jumping – this event horse moves well and has a good rider, but there is always the risk of injury.

Horses can enjoy letting off energy when turned out in a field or arena, but there is a fine line between protection and overprotection.

OVERPROTECTIVE?

Have we become overprotective of our horses? That's a question you have to answer by considering your individual horse or pony and his situation, but there may be times when barelegged is best.

It comes down to common sense: for instance, if you're jumping a cross-country course, the risk of injury demands that boots be worn. But if you're hacking out in muddy conditions, or out hunting for a few hours on an experienced horse, in country where little jumping is involved, boots might be counterproductive. If dirt gets trapped between the boot and the horse's leg for long periods, it can cause rubs and skin infections.

Some people fit boots at every opportunity, even when turning horses out. Again, it often pays to be selective. If he only goes out for short periods and tends to explode, boots might be a worthwhile precaution – though giving him more turnout time will usually make him happier and more sensible!

SIZE AND DESIGN

Boots are usually marketed in pony, cob and horse or small, medium and large sizes. However, they should be selected according to the horse's leg conformation, not his overall size.

Many Thoroughbreds tend to be longer in the cannon bone but relatively light of bone compared to a cob. Bone, usually used as an indication of a horse's weight-carrying ability, is measured just below the knee round the widest part of the cannon bone.

If the proportions of a boot don't match those of your horse's leg, they will slip, interfere with the flexion of his joints, or both. Forelegs have less bone and shorter cannon bones than hind legs.

MATERIALS AND FITTING

Traditionally, boots were made from leather, which provides good impact resistance but used to be difficult to care for – wet, muddy leather needs careful maintenance if it is not to harden and crack. But modern leather boots can be waterproof and easycare, and neoprene or detachable sheepskin linings make looking after them even easier.

There is also a huge range of lightweight, impact-resistant materials and others that incorporate an element of stretch. If you are choosing cross-country boots, an extra factor to consider will be what happens when they get wet: some materials may become waterlogged and heavy.

These tendon boots have three impact-resistant areas and a corrugated lining said to disperse impact.

Fastenings range from simple Velcro or similar hook-and-eye types to straps and buckles. Touch-and-close straps make for ease of use, but don't always stand up to frequent use on synthetic surfaces; in particular, sand tends to work its way in and cause straps to come undone, with obvious dangers.

They also tend to trap hair and pieces of bedding, so if it's safe to do so, put on and remove the boots when the horse is outside the stable. To prolong their stickability, keep straps closed when they are not in use or are being washed, and remove any bits that get trapped by using special Velcro combs, available from most saddlers.

Straps and buckles or slide fastenings are more time-consuming to put on and take off, but stay fastened. If you use touch-and-close fastenings, designs with double overlaying straps offer greater security.

The golden rule is that straps should be fastened so that the ends point towards the hind legs. This is not only because they are less likely to pull undone, but also because boots are designed to conform to the shape of the limbs when fastened this way round.

The latest boots, such as these Veredus Projump fetlock boots, are made from high-tech impact-resistant materials.

Equilibrium's Stretch and Flex training boots are close-fitting, with an element of stretch.

It also means that you usually need to identify which boot goes on which leg. One exception is a clever design for everyday use that can be used on any leg; it may sound like dumbing down, but there are times when idiot-proof designs are well worth having.

Boots should be put on so that the leg hair underneath them lies flat, so hold them a little above their eventual site and slide them down. They should be fastened tightly enough to keep them in place, which generally means that you should be able to slip a finger between the top and bottom of the boot and the horse's leg.

When putting on brushing and tendon boots, fasten the centre strap first (1), then the top one (2), followed by the bottom strap (3) and any others (4, 5). This helps to make sure tension is kept even. When removing them, undo the bottom strap first and work upwards to minimize the risk of the boot flapping if the horse moves and spooking him further.

Designs that go over the horse's foot (below) and protect the sole – either as a temporary measure when a shoe is lost, or as a permanent one, to protect thin soles – need very careful fitting. Even when every care is taken, some designs have a tendency to rub the heels. Applying a little petroleum jelly to clean heels may prevent this.

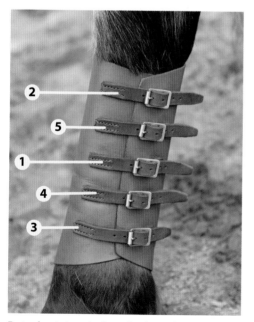

Fasten boot straps in the order shown here.

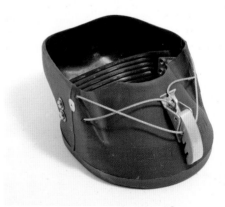

KNEE TO HEEL

The type of boot you choose depends on which area of the leg you are trying to protect and also on the job your horse is doing. For instance, boots that protect the tendon area are often used when jumping. If you need an all-round boot for general riding, well-designed brushing boots are a good option.

GIVING THE BRUSH-OFF

Brushing boots should have a reinforced strike pad down the cannon bone area. If the strike pad is stitched on to the main part of the boot, look for designs where the stitching is recessed (set into a groove) as this puts less wear and tear on the thread and the boots will last longer. Fetlock or ankle boots are shortened versions of brushing boots and, as their name suggests, protect only the fetlock area. They are sometimes favoured by show jumpers who want to protect the fetlock joints but believe that if a horse taps a pole with a 'bare leg' he is more likely to be careful.

A ring boot, which is a hollow rubber tube that takes a central connecting strap, is less commonly seen, but can be useful for horses who move on a single track behind. When you watch these horses move, you will see that they place their near hind foot in line with the offside one, instead of putting their hind feet down side by side.

You only need to use a single ring boot, which is fastened just below the fetlock joint. This design is sometimes confused with a sausage boot, which is thicker and softer and designed to prevent a horse striking his elbow with the heel of his shoe when he lies down or gets up after a snooze.

KNEES AND HOCKS

Some riders like to use knee boots when riding on the roads. The problem with most designs is that even when adjusted so that the top strap is tight enough to prevent slipping and the bottom strap is loose, to prevent interference with the joint, they may only stay in place at walk.

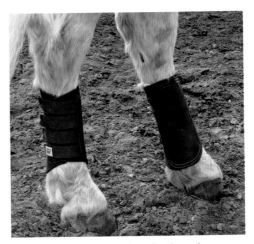

Brushing boots have a reinforced strike pad.

Knee boots give protection on the roads but are only suitable for slow work.

They are usually fine for travelling, if you wish to use them, but for riding, a boot that combines the protection of both brushing and knee boots is often better.

Hock boots can be used when travelling and some people use them in the stable to minimize the risk of capped hocks in horses who scrape away their bedding. Rubber matting is a safer option than leaving hock boots on overnight.

HEELS AND CORONETS

Overreach injuries on the back of the heel can be difficult to heal, as every time the horse takes a step the wound opens and closes. Although overreach (bell) boots are designed to prevent the horse hurting himself, opinions vary on the effectiveness of the various designs and even their safety.

Straightforward rubber boots are cheap but may invert. Other designs are shaped to stay in place without swivelling round the foot, so the risk of the horse treading on them is lessened. However, some people believe that if they have hardened inner inserts to prevent them rotating, there is a risk that when the horse lands over a fence, the angle of the fetlock joint may cause the inserts to put pressure on tendons and ligaments.

Petal boots, invented by UK designer Hilary Westropp and marketed under her name, are one of the safest designs because if the horse treads on the boot, the petals detach – hopefully affording protection first – and can be replaced. The original design was rather noisy, as the petals flapped up and down, but the updated one is much quieter.

Hock boots can be used when travelling or in the stable, but it's safer to use rubber matting than leave them overnight.

Westropp petal boots are perhaps the safest design on the market. If the horse treads on a boot and pulls off a petal, simply fit a replacement one.

> **TIP**
>
> Although boots are useful in preventing injury, it's important to call on your farrier's expertise. By altering the type of shoe used, he may be able to minimize the risks further.

PROTECTION AND SUPPORT

Tendon injuries are every horse-owner's nightmare, as they can permanently reduce or even end a horse's athletic capability. Although many are the result of a strain, they can also be caused by a hind foot striking the back of a foreleg, especially when jumping. Because of this, tendon boots are often regarded as standard protection, as the reinforced area down the back of the leg should deflect most blows. Closed-front designs give some protection to the rest of the leg, but show jumpers usually prefer open-fronted ones because they believe too much protection can make a horse careless over poles.

Closed-front tendon boots.

SUPPORT ACT

One of the big questions about tendon boots is whether they provide support as well as protection for horses recovering after tendon injury. An American study aimed at resolving conflicting evidence set out to discover whether they reduced tension on the superficial digital flexor tendon (SDFT), and involved 26 horses and four types of boot.

Front fetlock joint angles were measured while the horses were worked on a treadmill at walk and trot, with and without boots. The conclusion was that they reduced maximum extension of the fetlock – which the researchers assumed reduced tension in the SDFT – but they also pointed out that over a prolonged period, this might have a bad effect on fibre alignment in the healing tendon.

Some riders – particularly those in the Western disciplines – use boots with straps that cradle the fetlock and are said to help prevent the fetlock overextending. At the same time, the material has enough stretch to make sure movement is not restricted.

If tendon support is a priority for an animal in work, ask your vet's advice about whether you should use boots or exercise bandages.

It has to be said that boots are nearly always recommended, because if exercise bandages are applied unevenly, or too tightly, they can cause more problems than they prevent; the tendency nowadays is to use them only when there really is no alternative.

They are about 10cm (4in) wide and made from stretchy material; some have a fleece section which goes next to the leg and provides padding, followed by a longer stretch section. Like stable and travel bandages, they should be applied over a layer of extra padding, such as Fybagee.

Bandaging techniques and tips are explained on pages 144–5 in the section on travel and stable bandages, which are much more commonly used than exercise ones.

Raising the game

Can boots improve a horse's jumping performance? Some riders think so, and use weighted boots in practice or warm-up sessions to encourage the horse to pick up his feet better. Another design is said to encourage a horse to extend his quarters and hind legs over a fence.

Sadly, there have been incidents of riders using boots with projections on the inside, which prick the legs when the horse hits a fence. These are, not surprisingly, forbidden under international rules.

For safety's sake, the straps on these tendon boots should be shortened.

Western-style riders whose horses perform movements such as spins and sliding stops often prefer boots with straps that cradle the fetlock.

'Our international reining stallion, Whata Smoke, is fitted with "slicks" for competition – thin, extra-wide shoes that allow sliding stops without putting stress on the limbs. Because these have to be razor thin, he always competes in tendon and overreach boots.'
Sue Painter, chairman UK Paint Horse Association

OPTIONS FOR TRAVEL

In most cases, it's standard practice to protect a horse's legs when travelling. The notable exceptions are broodmares and foals – it would be impractical and potentially dangerous to apply boots or bandages to foals and they may be frightened by strange appendages suddenly appearing on their mothers' legs.

In any case, neither will be shod and so the risks are already minimized. Some owners take that further and believe that leg protection is unnecessary for any unshod animals.

In continental Europe, valuable horses are often travelled barelegged on international journeys, as handlers believe they are more comfortable that way. However, vehicle interiors are designed to minimize risks, with plenty of padding.

When leg protection is used, it must be robust but also comfortable, so the horse is not irritated and likely to kick. The main decision is whether to use boots or bandages: both have pros and cons.

Correctly applied bandages may be less likely to slip, but take longer to put on and remove; this may be a factor when travelling a young horse who is likely to be excited when he arrives at a competition, though there is a way round this (see opposite). If you want to give full protection to the knee and hock area, you may need to use knee and hock boots as well.

Travel boots are quicker to put on and remove, but unless they are well designed and suit your horse's leg conformation perfectly, they may slip. The best designs cover the knee and hock, though it is possible to use short travel boots combined with knee and hock boots.

Some horses shift their weight a lot when travelling and may literally tread on their own feet, pulling off a shoe or bruising a heel or coronet. Using a safe design of overreach boots all round, or boots with reinforced bottom sections to protect these areas, will minimize the risks.

Well-designed travel boots such as these, from the PolyPads range, are easy to put on and remove and don't slip.

Undo travel boot fastenings from the bottom up, so the boot doesn't slip and flap round the horse's leg.

'When you've put on your travel bandages, tape over the fastenings or stitch the end in place. You can then get straight on the horse when you arrive at the show and the bandages will provide protection while you work in.

When he's settled, you can then remove them and, if necessary, replace them with boots.'
Lynn Russell

STABLE BANDAGES AND BOOTS

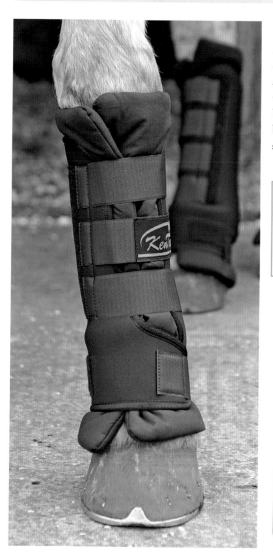

For an older and/or stiffer horse, or one who needs leg support, stable bandages or boots can offer extra comfort. Stable bandages are essentially the same as travel ones, but usually finish above the fetlock rather than below. Alternatively, you can buy stable boots or wraps, which are said to offer the same benefits.

Safety first

Never wet bandages, or they will tighten as they dry.

TIP

Instead of wrapping padding round the leg and holding it in place while you bandage, line up the bandage along the padding and apply both together, as shown on page 144.

These well-designed Kentaur stable boots are a good alternative to stable bandages.

Golden rules

1. Always apply over padding, which can range from cotton or felt-type materials to gel pads.
2. Start with the bandage rolled correctly so you finish with the fastenings on the outside.
3. Bandage from front to back to avoid putting pressure on tendons and ligaments.
4. Keep pressure even as you bandage down and then back up the leg.
5. Tapes or ties should be fastened on the outside of the leg, at the side – not at the back, where they could put pressure on the tendons, or at the front, where they could press on the cannon bone.
6. The bandage should be tight enough to stay in place, but you should be able to slip a finger in the top.

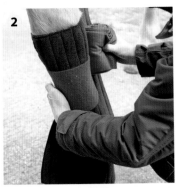

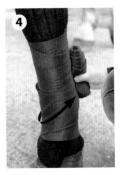

TAIL ENDINGS

Tail bandages are used to protect the hair when travelling and to keep a pulled or shaped tail looking neat. They are about 10cm (4in) wide and elasticated; their stretch quality helps keep them in place, but means they must be applied with care.

Some people like to use tailguards as well as, or instead of, tail bandages. These are usually designed for slimmer docks and won't always fit horses with fat docks, such as cobs, or thick, heavy tails, such as those of mountain and moorland ponies.

Although some people are happy to leave a tail bandage on their horse overnight, it is best to limit its application to just two or three hours' duration. There have been cases where tail hair has fallen out because the circulation has been affected by the bandage, and white hairs have grown through in place of dark colours.

To apply a tail bandage, ensure it is rolled the right way round with the tapes or fastening strap inside, then unroll 15–20cm (6–8in) and place it under the tail (1). Make your first turn, fold down the loose end and bandage over it – this will help prevent the bandage slipping (2).

Bandage down with even but not tight pressure until you reach the end of the dock, then wind the bandage back up the tail (3). Tie or fasten the tapes so that they are no tighter than the bandage itself and tuck in the ends. Folding the bandage over will help keep tie tapes out of the way (4), ensuring a neat and tidy finish.

Finally, bend the tail gently into its natural position (5).

QUESTIONS AND ANSWERS

Q My skewbald has a grey tail, and though it's clean when we set off for a show, it's always dirty by the time we get there. How can I keep the long hairs clean while travelling?

A The easiest and cheapest way of doing this is to cut the leg and foot from an old pair of tights and use this stretchy nylon tube to encase the tail. Bandage over the top of it in the normal way and you should find you arrive at the show with a pristine tail.

Alternatively, buy a tail bag – a nylon bag that does the same job. Some designs incorporate a tailguard.

Q My horse has white legs and sensitive skin, and all the boots I've tried rub him, even though I wash them every time they are used. Is there anything that will help?

A Professional grooms often use a little talcum powder on the linings of new boots to help prevent them rubbing. You could also look for boots with detachable, washable, sheepskin linings.

Q I've always travelled my horse using a nylon headcollar. A friend insists that this isn't safe – is she right, and if so, what is a safer option?

A If a horse panics when he is tied up, you need to be able to release him quickly. That isn't easy when he is in a horsebox, even though there is access from the driver's cab and/or living section to the horse accommodation – and it is impossible when he is in a trailer, as you have to stop the towing vehicle in a safe place, get out and access the horse through the trailer groom's door without hurting yourself.

The trouble with nylon headcollars is that they are by definition very strong and may not break in an emergency before cutting into the horse's head. It is safer to use a leather headcollar, which is strong enough for normal wear and tear but will break under unacceptable strain.

Made-to-measure leather headcollar.

Q My horse paws the ground when travelling and managed to bang his knee, even though the padding under his travelling bandages covered this area. Is there anything I can do to prevent this happening again?

A If you travel your horse without a haynet, giving him one may help him to settle and keep him occupied.

The hay should be soaked, or you should use haylage, to keep his environment as dust free as possible.

If you prefer to use travelling bandages, add a pair of knee boots. Alternatively, use boots that extend over the knee and have plenty of padding or reinforcement to minimize the risk of injury.

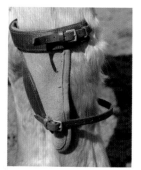

Knee boot.

PolyPad travel boots.

7

RUGS

CONTENTS

RUGGED OR OVER-RUGGED?

Look in any shop or catalogue and you'll see rugs for all seasons and all purposes. Thanks to modern fabric technology, you can now protect your horse against the elements, and against other hazards such as biting insects, all year round. You can also spend a small fortune doing so!

But although rugs can be essential for a horse or pony's comfort and protection, there are some instances when we need to be careful not to go too far the other way. For instance, native breeds such as Exmoors and Shetlands are designed to take the worst nature can throw at them, thanks to their body shape, thicker skin and thick coats, which stand on end and trap a layer of warm air next to the skin.

Of course, when we groom the natural protective grease from their coats and clip them so they can work without sweating, we have to replace what we've taken away. Rugs can then be essential: but if your horse or pony isn't working hard and has shelter from wind and rain, be circumspect about what you put on him.

The other side of the coin is that the right rugs can help horses who wouldn't otherwise be able to cope with bad weather to live out for longer periods, thus ensuring they aren't standing in a stable for most of the day. And if, like most owners, you have work and family commitments, it's much easier to remove a muddy rug and tack up a clean horse than to have to spend hours cleaning him up before you can ride.

'A horse will use up to 10 per cent of the energy from his food to keep warm, so rugging him up correctly will help save on feed bills. By the same token, an overweight horse ought to work off some of his excess fat by keeping warm!'
Dr Theresa Hollands, nutritionist for Dodson and Horrell

FIT FOR THE JOB

Rugs range from the most basic to state-of-the-art designs, but whether you're looking for a cheap turnout rug for a youngster who will outgrow it in six months or one made from the latest high-tech fabrics, it has to fit and be adjusted correctly.

That sounds obvious, but go round any yard and you'll see horses with rugs that have slipped back or over to one side, restricting movement and causing rubs and discomfort. Manufacturers say that the most common mistake is to buy a rug that is too large in the mistaken impression that it will give the wearer more protection. As the length increases, so do the other proportions – so the neck length as well as the body length will be greater and the rug will be more likely to slip.

To find the right-size stable or turnout rug for your horse, take a basic measurement from the centre of his chest, along his body to a point where a vertical line dropped from the top of his tail would fall. To give a more detailed picture, you can also measure from just behind the withers to below the belly line, where the bottom edge of the rug would fall, and from 10cm (4in) in front of the withers to the top of the tail.

Exercise rug.

Exercise rugs are either measured along the centre back line or sold as small, medium and large.

In general, you get what you pay for. Rugs in the medium and upper price brackets usually have more shaping and better-quality fastenings and are made from better-quality fabrics.

The basic measurement used to find the correct size of stable or turnout rug goes from the centre of the chest, along the body to the point where a vertical line dropped from the top of his tail would fall.

HOW MANY?

It's easy to spend a fortune on rugs, but multi-purpose designs can help you save money. If you're starting from scratch, or have a youngster who is going to outgrow them by next season, you may be able to get away with two or three breathable turnout rugs, as many designs can be used indoors as well as out.

They also tend to have tougher outer layers, which makes them especially useful for hooligans, and are fairly easy to keep clean.

For the horse who lives out all the time, opting for one lightweight and two medium-weight designs allows you to choose according to weather conditions. For the horse kept on a combined system, a choice of three allows you to keep one primarily for indoor use, so you won't have mud drying and spreading dust into the stable environment.

Make sure you always have a dry, weatherproof rug ready for use so that you have a spare if one gets damaged. Most lightweight and some medium-weight designs fit into domestic washing machines and you can cut down washing and drying time further by using a cotton summer sheet or lightweight fleece underneath – cheap to buy, they save you having to wash your top rug so often and mean there is a clean layer next to your horse's skin and coat.

Another item that should be added to your essentials shopping list as soon as possible is a thermal rug or cooler, which transfers moisture from the horse's body to the outer layer of the fabric.

TIP

Most shops will let you try on a rug and exchange it if it is the wrong size, provided it is kept clean. The best way to ensure this is to try it on over a cotton summer sheet or, if your horse isn't too spooky, an old bed sheet.

Breathable turnout rug.

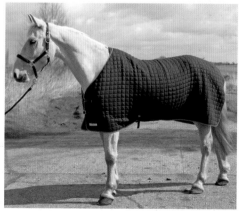

Thermatex thermal rug.

SHAPING UP

Horses, like people, come in different shapes and sizes. Height often has very little to do with the size of rug needed: a broad 15hh (152cm) cob may need the same size rug as a 16.2hh (168cm) Thoroughbred. And as rugs are designed for a standard conformation blueprint, horses who don't quite fit within its parameters may be more difficult to suit, though there are ways round most problems.

For instance, if your horse has a particularly wide chest, look for fabrics that incorporate an element of stretch, or see if the manufacturer includes a chest expander in its range. This is a rectangle of fabric with fastenings that bridge the gap where it's needed.

Horses with particularly sloping shoulders and long strides are often best suited in rugs with shoulder gussets, which allow for extra movement. If your horse is straighter in the shoulder than ideal and rugs tend to gape or rub, try a stretch 'body' or shoulder vest underneath.

FASTENINGS AND ADJUSTMENT

Good-quality fastenings are as important as good-quality fabrics. You don't have to be a metallurgist to see the difference between superior and not so good clips and buckles – quality shows in the finish and ease of use. For instance, cheap clips often don't work smoothly from the start and may break, whereas top-quality ones last for years.

Outdoor and stable rugs are usually secured by T-bars or buckles and straps at the centre chest – though some manufacturers believe it is better to fasten them at the shoulder – and by cross surcingles or under-belly harnesses. Stretch designs may have zips or may pass over the horse's head; most accept this if they are introduced carefully.

You should be able to fit a hand's-width between the front of the rug and the horse's chest. Cross surcingles should cross in the centre of the horse's belly and these too should be adjusted to allow a hand's-width between them and the horse's body.

Chest expander.

The Dress Circle Horsewear Sherpa rug is breathable and avoids the risk of rubs.

Some rugs have rear legstraps. These are usually linked, whereas front legstraps, which are less commonly seen, are not. Again, allow a hand's-width between the strap and the horse's leg.

Under-belly harnesses keep the rug in place without the risk of pressure on the spine or withers. This won't happen with cross surcingles on a well-designed rug, but can occur if the surcingles are attached too high or are on, rather than just behind, the shoulder.

With all fastenings, follow the manufacturer's fitting guidelines. This is especially important with harnesses, as fixing methods vary and if they are too loose, there is a risk that a horse could catch up a leg after rolling or lying down.

Safety first

People often complain that a rug has torn or that a fastening has broken while their horse is out in the field. However, every rug must have a breaking point, because if your horse gets caught up on something and the rug doesn't break, his leg or neck might.

Allow a hand's-width between cross surcingles and the horse's belly and between the front of the rug and his chest. If the rug is the correct size, this will keep it in place without it rubbing or slipping.

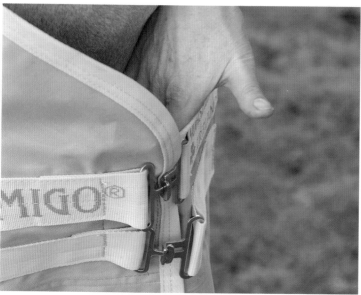

MATERIAL BENEFITS

Fabric technology means today's rugs are light years ahead of those of even ten years ago. You can now have warmth and waterproof qualities without weight – a big consideration for owners struggling to rug-up large horses as well as being more comfortable for the horses themselves – and fabrics which contribute to multi-functional rugs.

Ballistic nylon, which is used in bulletproof vests, is one favourite for outer fabrics. Ripstop fabrics are another; ripstop is a type of weave with small squares which helps contain the extent of any tear.

Ordinary-looking materials often have extraordinary qualities. For instance, some manufacturers use hydrophilic (water-loving) coatings on the underside.

These coatings prevent water passing through from the outside, but use the temperature difference between the horse and the air to allow sweat to travel through from the horse to the outside of the rug, where it evaporates. Aluminium coatings are used to reflect body heat inwards.

The inside of a rug is as important as the outside. At least one company now uses fabric that incorporates silver, which is used to combat MRSA in hospitals and is said to help prevent skin infections.

Some rugs have slippery nylon linings that help prevent rubs and also polish the coat, but on rare occasions, they can produce static electricity.

Travelling horses can present a challenge, especially on long journeys and in changeable weather. We all appreciate the importance of well-ventilated vehicles and the need, at the same time, to protect horses from draughts to avoid muscle cramps. This used to mean carrying several rugs so that you could cater for all weather conditions.

Thermal fabrics use a fabric sandwich to keep horses warm and dry without the risk of overheating, all within a lightweight rug that's easy to wash and handle. The outside and inside layers comprise wool, or wool and manmade knitted fibres, with a filling of textured polypropylene to provide insulation.

The horse's body heat pushes moisture to the outside, where it evaporates; you can see the droplets beading on the outer surface, while the horse dries off underneath. As with many other high-tech rugs, the beauty of these designs is that they can be put straight on to a wet or sweating horse.

Ripstop fabric.

FAL Pro rugs incorporate silver.

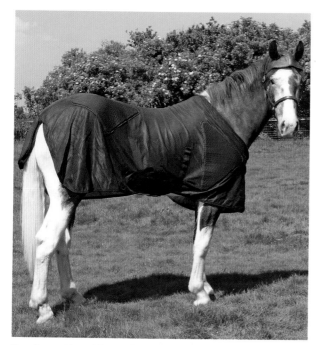

Travel rug with padding on hips and shoulders.

If your problem is a horse who bangs his shoulder or hips against the partitions, which can happen with inexperienced animals even when the horsebox or towing outfit is set up correctly and driven considerately, look for rugs which offer extra protection with padding on these vulnerable areas.

Breathable, waterproof fabrics have also revolutionized exercise sheets. If you're planning to hack out and compete through the winter, it's easier than it's ever been to make sure your horse's muscles stay warm; designs that fasten round the saddle rather than going underneath mean that waiting in draughty collecting rings is no longer a risk, as you can leave a rug on a clipped horse until the last minute.

Exercise rugs that fasten round the saddle are more efficient.

KEEPING COOL

Rugs can be a real boon when you need to cool down or dry off a horse without him getting a chill. If possible, it's best to keep him walking rather than trust a rug to do it all for you – but if for some reason this isn't possible, a lightweight thermal or cooler rug will be invaluable.

It's still possible to buy traditional large-mesh anti-sweat rugs, which are the equine equivalent of, and work on the same principle as, old-fashioned string vests. They do work – though only if used correctly with another rug on top and, even then, not as efficiently as modern fabrics.

Using two rugs traps a layer of warm air created by a mixture of moisture and the horse's body heat. Mesh anti-sweat rugs can also be used for the old-fashioned practice of 'thatching', where a layer of dry hay is spread over a wet horse's back and the rug secured over it. The horse will dry off and keep reasonably warm at the same time, but it's a long process.

Small-mesh fabrics continue to be popular and some rugs made from these are said to be efficient when used alone.

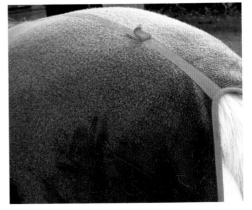

Lightweight thermal fabric by Thermatex transfers moisture to the outside.

Stretch velour cooler by Horseware.

Other modern alternatives include lightweight fleeces and thermal knit fabrics with wicking properties – in other words, moisture is drawn from the horse's coat and skin through the fabric to the surface. 'Fleece' is actually a misnomer, as most fleeces are not made from sheep's wool but from synthetic fibres.

Cotton is also often used in coolers, as it is both absorbent and breathable. It is frequently combined with polyester to give extra durability.

If you're looking for glamour as well as practicality, there are now fleeces with a velour finish as well as ones incorporating gold thread!

Safety first

Most coolers have either cross surcingles or a strap that fastens under the belly and should be safe to leave on a horse in the stable. However, if you use a design that has only a chest fastening, you will need to use an elasticated surcingle or a roller to keep it in place – if the horse rolls, he could get his leg caught in the fabric, leading possibly to injury and certainly to a ruined rug.

ICE-COOL

Research into the effects of heat and humidity has shown that rapid cooling can be a safe way to lower a horse's core body temperature. Research has shown that during hard exercise in normal conditions – or even low-to-moderate exercise when it's hot and humid – heat production can increase by up to 50 per cent.

In response, a horse may produce more sweat than evaporation can disperse, so his natural thermoregulation system runs into problems. A new system to combat these problems combines a lightweight rug and a cooling fluid used to coat it.

This is a new-generation mesh anti-sweat rug; the cooling fluid is used to coat the fabric and when the rug is placed on the horse, his muscles are cooled more quickly and recovery time is said to speed up. The fluid doesn't have to be refrigerated and is said to contain no substances that are banned or restricted under international competition rules.

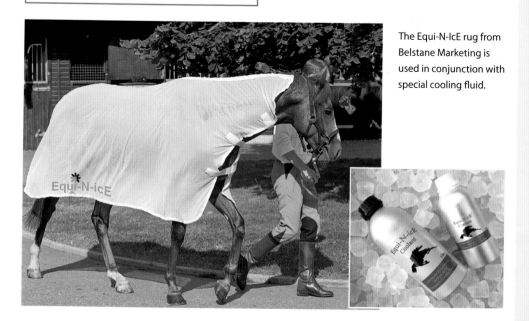

The Equi-N-IcE rug from Belstane Marketing is used in conjunction with special cooling fluid.

QUESTIONS AND ANSWERS

Q Even though they're adjusted correctly, the cross surcingles on my horse's rug keep coming undone. Is there anything that I can do to prevent this?

A Look for tiny rubber 'doughnuts' that fit over the T-bar and prevent it slipping round and coming undone when your horse rolls. A small rubber band wound round the bar will do the same job, but the doughnuts are cheap and easy to use.

Q I need to use a rug with a neck cover so that my horse stays reasonably clean, but he has very high withers and there are signs of rubbing at the base of his mane. How can I get round this?

A There are two ways to help prevent rubbing. One is to use a rug with a detachable neck cover (below) rather than one with a neck cover built in, as this allows more movement when your horse puts his head down to graze. The other is to use a stretch hood (below right) or, if you don't want to cover his face, a neck cover with earholes that extends just below the base of the ears.

Q My horse is fully clipped and I use a horse walker for warming up and cooling down. He gets too warm under his lightweight stable rug but isn't warm enough without a rug. It isn't safe to put him on the horse walker wearing a saddle and exercise rug – are there any rugs that would solve this problem?

A Some manufacturers now make designs especially for use on horse walkers, with cutaway shoulders. These keep the horse warm but don't restrict movement. Alternatively, if the design of your walker means it is safe to use an ordinary rug, a lightweight fleece design might work.

Q My horse is very difficult to clip. Is there any way I can prevent his winter coat coming through too quickly without having to put on too many rugs?

A You need a stretch fleece cover-up set made from lightweight, breathable material. This will inhibit coat growth without him getting too hot.

Q My two-year-old lives out at a DIY livery yard and needs rugs in the winter. He's a real hooligan and damages rugs playing with his friends. As he's also growing rapidly, I thought I could save money by buying second-hand rugs. Are there any precautions I should take?

A The risk with buying second-hand rugs – unless you know for certain that they have only had one previous, infection-free wearer – is that they may harbour ringworm spores. Although ringworm isn't dangerous, it is an inconvenience and you would not be popular if you introduced it to your yard.

It's sensible to have any second-hand rugs, even those from a known source, washed by a professional rug-washing company and to wipe them over or spray them before use with a preparation that is guaranteed to kill off ringworm spores but that won't damage the fabric.

Q I have a 17.3hh (180cm) Warmblood and although I can find rugs that are long enough and fit well round the chest and shoulders, they are never deep enough through the girth. What can I do to keep him warm enough when he is clipped?

A Try using a stretch body suit under your rug, as this would cover the belly area. Alternatively, some manufacturers will make rugs to your horse's measurements.

8

HEALTH AND SAFETY

CONTENTS

INVEST TO PROTECT

Whether you are a professional competition rider or someone who keeps a horse purely for pleasure, your management and riding techniques need to focus on his well-being and safety. In turn, this will often benefit you.

For instance, keeping him sound and supple will enable him to work more efficiently and thus bring you more pleasure and success. More importantly, making sure you are seen easily by other road users could save both your lives. In these and other scenarios, the right equipment can make a real difference.

This can range from the simple to the high-tech and from the scientifically proven to that offering benefits supported only by anecdotal evidence. As in the field of human medicine, it isn't always possible to prove why something such as magnetic therapy works, but we do know that many horses seem to benefit from it. However, if you're looking for equipment to improve your horse's well-being and think he may have a health problem, always start by getting your vet's advice. In some cases, it's also important to check that whatever you plan to use can't have a detrimental effect.

It is also important to protect and safeguard your tack and equipment. Routine care and security measures take relatively little time and money, but will repay you many times over.

Anti-fly rugs can reduce irritation from insects.

Massage can be hands-on or high-tech.

GETTING A GRIP

Whatever a horse's job, he needs to get a grip. For some disciplines, particularly eventing and show jumping, studs are an essential part of most riders' equipment, but they are only part of the picture, and even those who use them as standard emphasize that safety is as important as security.

They can't work miracles. For instance, small studs might give a dressage horse competing on grass more confidence in his movement, but they won't compensate for a horse being on his forehand or incorrectly ridden.

STUD TACTICS

There is a huge range of designs available, but general guidelines are that pointed studs are for hard going and rounded ones for soft. Always use the smallest size possible, as the larger the stud, the greater the risk that the horse might strike himself with it; it's essential to use protective boots when you are using studs.

Opinions vary on whether it's best to use one or two studs in each shoe. However, the favourite approach of many top riders is to use two on each hind shoe and one or two on each front shoe.

If slippery road surfaces are a problem, ask your farrier's advice about the best approach to take. This could mean using special road studs, perhaps in just the hind shoes. The horse's foot should always be able to move slightly when it meets the ground, to help absorb shock.

Always use a studguard when jumping a horse who has studs fitted, so that if he strikes into the girth area, he doesn't injure himself.

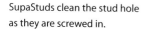

SupaStuds clean the stud hole
as they are screwed in.

Use pointed studs for hard
ground and rounded ones
for soft.

Clean mud and grit from stud holes with a horseshoe
nail, and plug the cleared holes; the traditional choice for
this is cotton-wool plugs soaked in hoof oil or WD-40.
Alternatively, special 'blanks' or 'travel studs' can be used
for short periods only; if used for long periods, there is a risk
that they may become difficult to remove.

With standard designs, you need to clear the thread with
a screw tap – sometimes called a T-tap – every time you
refit studs, and secure them with a spanner, which is usually
built into the T-tap handle. However, there are now studs
available that clean the thread as they are applied.

TIP
It's easy to drop a stud and lose
it, especially when at an outdoor
competition. Magnetic wristbands
allow you to keep them safe.

Going the distance
Endurance riders avoid studs because they are riding for
long distances and often cover several kinds of terrain on
one ride. However, a specialist farrier may suggest shoeing a
horse slightly tighter than usual for competition, particularly
in front – in other words, shoeing to the outline of the foot
and not beyond so that the shoes stay secure.

*'I don't use studs when schooling at home – when I'm never going to be
under the same pressure as in competition – because I don't want my
horses to rely on them. When the ground is hard and slippery or the going is
particularly deep, I'll use two small studs on either side of the shoe.'*
Andrew Nicholson, member of the New Zealand three-day event team

NOT-SO-SEASONAL PROBLEMS

It's often assumed that different times of year present different problems and potential hazards for horses. To a certain extent this is true, but climate change means that some dangers can lurk nearly all year round.

For instance, mild, wet autumns and winters mean that grass continues to grow for longer periods and that nutrients remain at higher levels. This means that laminitis is no longer a problem just in spring and early autumn – last year, UK vets reported an alarming number of incidents during winter months.

Warm, wet weather also helps insects to thrive, so sweet itch can also be a long-lasting problem. Also, where there is rain, there is mud – and where there is mud, there is also mud fever.

Although there is no substitute for good management, the right equipment can help make both your and your horse's life easier.

The biggest dangers come from irritation caused by biting insects and also from your horse eating too much grass when nutrient levels are at their highest.

Horses and their surroundings are magnets to insects, which spread disease and infection. As well as making sure you maintain good hygiene, removing droppings as often as possible and keeping water containers clean, you can keep your horse more comfortable by using rugs and face masks.

Most anti-fly rugs are made from fine, tough mesh and often have detachable or built-in neck covers and belly straps. They offer good protection from larger insects, but if your horse suffers from sweet itch, an 'ordinary' anti-fly rug won't be enough.

Anti-fly rugs made from fine, tough mesh offer good protection from larger insects.

SWEET ITCH

Sweet itch is a distressing condition, and sufferers can rub their skin raw. It is now generally agreed that it is an allergic reaction to the saliva of a biting midge called *Culicoides*.

One of the best defences, along with a good management routine, is a specialized rug made from breathable fabric that the midges can't bite through but which doesn't cause overheating. Such rugs can be worn continuously and although most people remove them for riding, some designs can be left on during high-risk periods.

One of the original designs, the Boett blanket, comprises two pieces; one covers the neck, the body and the top of the tail, and the other is an adjustable belly band that goes over the body piece and fastens with elastic cross surcingles and a chest strap. A separate hood with ear covers is available for horses who show sweet itch reactions on the head area. Another design to combat *Culicoides*, from Snuggy Hoods, can include cover-ups for legs and udders.

Above and below: The Snuggy Hoods Sweet Itch Body and attachments can offer head-to-tail protection.

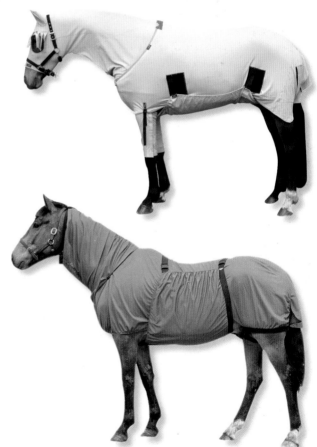

The Boett blanket is a two-piece set with adjustable belly band.

Flies and insects often settle round horses' eyes, because they are attracted by the moist membranes. This can soon lead to infection, so protective masks are essential at times in some areas.

Masks and leg wraps that provide UV protection can also prevent sunburnt muzzles and legs, often a problem in horses with pink skin.

Protective mask.

HEAD SHAKING

Another frequently seasonal problem is also distressing. Head shaking, where the horse makes jerky movements of the nose – and in the worst cases, may strike at his nose with a forefoot – has a profound effect on performance and can make some animals become unrideable.

There are many suggested causes, ranging from allergies and reactions to insects to swelling of blood vessels in the nose during exercise. Although every case is different and must be investigated by your vet, research at De Montfort University in the UK showed that the Equilibrium Net Relief muzzle net improved symptoms in nearly 80 per cent of test cases.

Because the net doesn't fully cover the muzzle, the horse is able to salivate freely and breathing is not restricted. It is currently permitted under UK competition rules, but, sadly, not under FEI regulations.

Equilibrium Net Relief muzzle net.

LAMINITIS

When grass is at its most nutritious, a period that can now extend from spring through to early winter, it can be difficult to provide sufficient turnout time without the risk of the horse or pony overeating. Apart from the risk of obesity, which puts strain on limbs and vital organs, there is also the threat of crippling laminitis in susceptible animals.

Grazing muzzles, which limit the intake of grass but don't interfere with drinking, can help, but some owners report problems with horses accepting these. Try feeding the horse by hand until he gets the idea.

Limiting grazing can be a problem.

NOT-SO-GLORIOUS MUD

Mud fever, a skin infection caused by a bacterium that can enter via the tiniest scratch, can make horses' and owners' lives a misery. It's often recommended that the legs of susceptible animals are clipped and that they are stabled as much as possible, but that isn't always possible and most people want their horses to be outdoors, not indoors.

A new generation of leg protectors may help. Some have wicking properties and are designed to be used to dry off legs quickly, and others form barriers between the mud and the horse.

Opinions vary as to whether mud should be washed off the legs, or left to dry and then brushed off. Unless your vet recommends otherwise, the best method is usually to hose off the mud with cold water, then pat dry with a clean towel and apply drying-off wraps. Don't use warm water, as this will open up the pores of the skin, and don't rub the legs as you hose off the mud, or you may cause abrasions that will admit the bacterium.

Turnout chaps or boots need to combine strength with stretch and it's vital to get the right size. If they are too small, they will cause pressure points and if they are too large, dirt will work in between the material and the horse's legs and make the problem worse.

Equi-Chaps from Equilibrium Products can reduce the risk of mud fever.

Horses with feathers (long hair) on their legs may be more susceptible to mud fever and need special care.

STABLE PROBLEMS

Stereotypic behaviour, once unfairly labelled 'stable vices', can be a physical concern as well as a mental one. Apart from the fact that horses carry out weaving, crib-biting and wind-sucking behaviours to try to relieve mental stress, there is the risk that a horse who weaves badly will put strain on his front legs and that one who crib-bites and/or wind-sucks may be more prone to colic.

WEAVING

The obvious answer with a weaver is to turn him out, as it is extremely rare to see a horse weaving outside. When horses have to be stabled, anti-weaving grilles – V-shaped grilles that fit on the stable door – may stop the behaviour in mild cases, but some horses will simply stand behind them and carry on.

Stallguards – barriers that fit across an open doorway – are often much more successful and most horses accept them. However, they should only be used when the horse is in sight, in case he does try to get out.

An anti-weaving grille may help in mild cases.

CRIB-BITING

Old-fashioned cribbing collars are, quite honestly, inhumane. They have a metal loop which presses into the horse's throat, causing pain when he arches his neck to grip the door or other surface, and have to be removed before the horse can eat or drink.

Another idea, fitting an electrified strip across the doorway so that the horse receives a mild shock when he tries to crib, would also be unacceptable to most people. If you have to limit

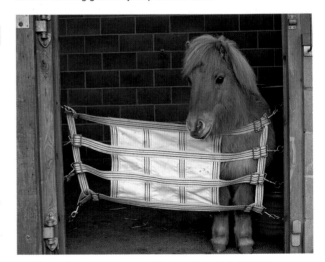

A stallguard can help keep a stabled horse or pony content.

cribbing to prevent damage to stables or fencing, a design patented as the Miracle Collar is generally regarded as a humane solution.

It has one strap that fastens in front of the ears and another that is secured just behind them and is said to apply enough pressure to discourage the horse when he goes to crib, but to allow him to eat and drink comfortably.

MIRROR, MIRROR

Stable mirrors have been shown to reduce anxiety and stereotypic behaviour, and some designs can also be used when travelling. The theory behind them is that horses are herd animals and some seem to take comfort from seeing their reflection.

If you want to use a stable mirror for a stallion, introduce it carefully. Some accept it calmly and react well, but there have been reports of stallions regarding the reflection as a rival, and showing aggression towards it.

Another way of keeping horses happy is to install grilles between stables so they can see each other.

FOOD FOR THOUGHT

Researchers generally agree that horses exhibit stereotypic behaviour to create endorphins: 'feel-good' chemicals produced naturally in the body. Preventing your horse doing this may cause more stress than allowing the behaviour, so weigh up all the pros and cons before deciding what to use.

Sometimes, compromise can be the best answer. A horse who cribs will cause less damage to his stable and his teeth if a section of old car tyre is fastened over the top of the stable door, giving him a soft surface to grip.

Horses who exhibit stereotypic behaviour and have to be stabled should be given ad-lib forage. Some crib-biters are said to reduce the behaviour when given an antacid supplement, so consult your vet for advice.

The Miracle Collar is regarded as more humane than traditional designs aimed at preventing horses from cribbing.

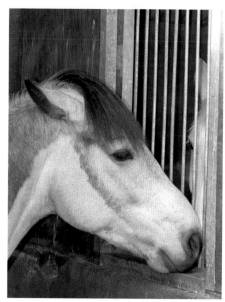

When shared air space is not a problem, a dividing grille helps keep horses happy.

'I had a stallion who weaved so badly behind a grille he knocked his eyes. My vet suggested I try a stable mirror and he became much calmer.'
Tim Stockdale, UK international show jumper

STAYING IN SIGHT

High-vis gear for horse and rider is vital whether you live in the UK, USA, Australia, or just about anywhere else in the world. However, specific requirements vary according to riding conditions and tradition.

Yellow and pink fluorescent gear is effective when riding out in daylight hours.

In the UK, where most riders exercise on the roads during daylight hours, yellow or pink fluorescent gear is most effective, as it shows up in all weather conditions. In the USA, there is much less roadwork except in city areas and even then it usually involves short distances between stables and riding areas.

However, American riders in country areas face a different danger: during the hunting season, riders are in real danger of being shot. For this reason, high-vis gear is vital, and orange is the accepted colour for hunters to watch out for.

In Australia, riders are likely to exercise at the very beginning or end of the day when conditions are cooler. This often means riding in the dark, so equipment needs to be highly reflective.

Wherever you live, the sensible option is to take a belt-and-braces approach and use equipment that is both reflective and fluorescent and to kit out horse and rider.

The American rider's orange safety wear makes him highly visible.

Riding without safety wear in the hunting season means risking your life.

When equipping a horse, make sure he can be seen from all directions. Research shows that in more than a third of UK road accidents involving horses, impact is from the rear, but high-vis rider gear coupled with high-vis horse gear at different heights gives the most effective warning.

Research at the Cranfield Institute of Technology in the UK showed that high-vis horse boots or leg straps are extremely effective, as the movement of the horse's legs attracts drivers' attention. At the front end, equipment available includes high-vis breastplates and martingales, and wraparounds for bridles and reins; at the sides and rear, an exercise sheet is most effective.

Modern fabrics mean that high-vis gear can be as flexible, non-rustling and easy to care for as any other. There are also belts and tabards with flashing lights as well as standard stirrup lights.

Although this book focuses on tack and equipment, what you wear is half the picture. If you want to keep safety gear to the minimum, the Cranfield Institute of Technology showed that the most effective combination was a rider tabard or Sam Browne belt and brushing boots on the horse.

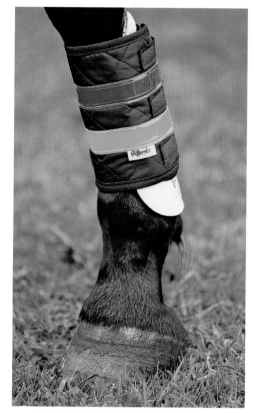

Boots with fluorescent, reflective leg bands catch the eye as the horse moves.

TIP

It can pay to have different colours in different seasons. Yellow is effective at most times of year, but in autumn, when leaves are turning yellow and orange, pink can be seen more clearly.

'If you're going to use a martingale, brushing boots or an exercise rug, make it high-vis. Safety doesn't have to be an extra – it can be incorporated into what you normally use. And make sure it's easy to clean; if you have to put it in the washing machine every time you use it, you probably won't, but if it can be rinsed under the tap, you probably will.'
Fiona Kennedy, high-vis clothing specialist

MAGNETS AND MASSAGE

The use of magnetic and massage therapies for humans and animals is increasingly popular. They are no longer regarded as 'touchy-feely' options, but as ways of promoting well-being and healing.

MAGNETS

Magnetic therapy is said to increase circulation and thus have a healing effect. The magnetic field improves the transfer of substances through the blood cells, speeding up the delivery of oxygen and nutrients and at the same time helping the removal of toxins via the lymph system.

There are two kinds of magnetic field: a pulsed electromagnetic field, which needs a supply of electricity, and a static one, which doesn't. Research using thermography (heat scanning) and scintigraphy (which uses radioactive markers) shows that the beneficial effects are genuine and not imagined; thermography has been used to measure an increase in blood flow and scintigraphy has demonstrated a significant increase in the rate at which substances taken into the soft tissue are taken up by the body.

In some situations, the need for electricity means that pulsed electromagnetic field therapy (PEMFT) is not practical. This is when static field products, such as rugs, boots and leg wraps, may be useful.

So when can magnetic therapy help? If improved circulation would benefit a condition, it could be worth trying if your vet approves, so candidates include horses suffering from ligament and tendon injuries, those who have newly formed splints, and older, stiffer animals who could benefit from increased blood flow before exercise.

Rugs incorporating static magnets are said to encourage muscle relaxation and therefore may also have a calming effect. The Equilibrium magnetic back pad offers the same benefits in a smaller, cheaper package that can be used on any size of horse.

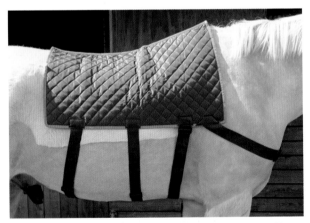

The Equilibrium magnetic back pad can be used on any size of horse and the magnets can be positioned to suit individual needs.

Magnets have also been incorporated into the Barnsby FTS headpiece, which is said to benefit both excitable and stiff horses.

Using a magnetic rug or back pads for about half an hour before riding stimulates blood flow to the muscles and starts the loosening-up process. They are an aid to warming up, but not a substitute for it, and you should still allow time for work on a loose rein where the horse is encouraged to stretch down.

Leg wraps and boots can be left on for longer periods and there are boots shaped to fit round knees, hocks and pasterns. Some owners leave them on overnight, but get veterinary advice on a regime to suit your horse's individual needs.

Don't use magnetic products when travelling. Increased blood flow means the horse could become too hot, even in a well-ventilated vehicle.

Barnsby FTS magnetic headpiece.

Safety first

If your horse has a problem, it's vital to get veterinary help first. Opinions vary as to whether there are instances where magnetic therapy should not be used; for instance, some practitioners say it should not be used on pregnant mares or on haematomas, whereas others believe that this applies only to PEMFT.

MASSAGE

Massage is another useful aid to well-being and equipment can range from a simple rubber groomer with soft prongs, used in a circular motion over the coat, to high-tech ways of stimulating circulation and encouraging healing.

Leather strapping pads can be used in conjunction with correct work and feeding to build up muscles. The pad should be brought down quite hard on the targeted area – neck or quarters, but never loins – so that the muscles twitch in anticipation. As long as you start gently and give the horse time to get used to it, most of them come to enjoy the process.

At the other end of the scale, the Equissage massage system provides deep-acting massage said to help a variety of conditions such as haematomas and stiffness associated with arthritis. It is used via a pad that straps on to the saddle or breast area, a handheld unit or a boot; for general well-being, the pad can be used for about 20 minutes each day.

The Equilibrium massage back pad is a new idea. It has three settings; low for cooling down, medium for warming up and high to help with some back problems.

Simple groomer.

The deep-acting Equissage massage system.

SAFETY AND SECURITY

Tack safety checks take only a few minutes, but could prevent a serious accident – remember that girths and stirrup leathers in particular take a lot of stress and that all leather, stitching and metalwork is subject to wear and tear.

Get into the habit of making a quick visual check every time before you mount any horse. When you clean your tack thoroughly each week (see pages 178–9) make a hands-on check to spot potential weak points.

The commonest weak points are stitching, turns – such as where leather is turned and sewn to take a buckle – areas round holes, and anywhere metal rests on leather. To check stitching, pull hard, especially on stirrup leathers, which have to bear a lot of weight.

Bridle stitching is also vulnerable and if billet fastenings are used, make sure the holes in the billet-place covers have not enlarged so that the billet itself is loose. Similarly, all buckle holes on your tack should be monitored for signs of enlargement and splits.

If you use a bridle or reins with plastic snap fastenings, as found on some synthetic bridles, or metal clip hooks, make sure they open and close freely.

Girths should be checked where leather turns through buckles. Try to use girths with rollers on the buckles, as these slide up the girth straps without cutting into the leather. On your saddle, check girth straps for wear and tear and make sure the webbing attachments are in good condition.

Good-quality leather that is well cared for will stay supple. Leather that has been allowed to become brittle will crack and split, and as soon as that happens, it is too weak to be safe.

Make sure billets are secure.

Check areas where leather is turned and sewn to take a buckle.

TIP
Synthetic tack is, in general, hard-wearing. But don't be lulled into a false sense of security – stitching is just as vulnerable as on leather tack.

Check that girth straps and attachments are in good condition.

SECURITY MEASURES

Tack theft is big business, so make sure yours can be identified by marking it with symbols that link it to your address, such as the UK postcode. Some saddle manufacturers implant microchips, but although this may be a useful back-up, police say that visible deterrents are more effective.

The best way to mark leather is with a 9mm (⅜in) die stamp. Wet the leather first, as this softens it, and when it dries, the mark is sharper than if it had been stamped into dry leather.

It's also a good idea to mark metalwork with your postcode or other identity symbol. Simple engravers are inexpensive and, with a bit of practice, are easy to use. You can mark stirrup bars, bit rings, stirrup irons and even buckles.

It's also worth displaying signs that all equipment on the premises is security marked.

Engrave metalwork with your postcode or other symbols that link it to your address.

TIP

There are thieves who will literally steal a rug off a horse's back – which, apart from the replacement cost, is serious when a clipped horse is turned out in bad weather. Writing your postcode or similar on a rug in large letters, using a broad, felt-tipped pen containing ink that doesn't wash off, is a good deterrent.

CLEANING UP

Properly looked after, good-quality leather tack will last for many years. If you buy new tack, look for any manufacturers' instructions, as some leathers have special finishes – for instance, waterproof leather should not be treated with anything other than recommended conditioners.

Although modern synthetic tack may look like leather, it could be ruined if you apply leather-care products. Again, follow the manufacturers' instructions.

In an ideal world, leather tack would be dismantled and thoroughly cleaned after every use. Realistically, few people have the time to do that, but as long as you make sure it isn't left wet and muddy, a thorough cleaning once a week, as described on pages 178–9, will keep it in good condition.

However, for the sake of your horse's health, there are some tasks that should be carried out every time you ride and that only take a minute or two.

Before you ride, make sure all the parts of your horse where tack rests are clean, so that mud isn't rubbed into the skin. After you've ridden, rinse the bit in clean water or use a bit wipe. If you leave it, dried saliva and perhaps food particles will harden on it and could rub the corners of his mouth.

It's also important to make sure that boots, numnahs or pads and girths are kept clean, since if dirt and sweat build up it can cause skin infections. They may not need cleaning or washing every day, but take damp numnahs and girths off the saddle and leave to dry.

Clean a bit every time it is used, either by rinsing in clean water or using a bit wipe, as shown here.

Use a Velcro brush to keep Velcro and other hook and eye fastenings free from debris.

WIPE IT OFF

Tack wipes impregnated with leather cleaner allow a speedy once-over after riding or before going into a competition. You can also get special bit wipes, including ones impregnated with peppermint and other flavours, which are said to encourage acceptance of the bit.

EMERGENCY MEASURES

When leather tack gets wet and/or muddy, it must be cleaned as soon as it's removed, and dried carefully. Don't soak it, or it may stretch. If necessary, use a small nailbrush to remove mud from leather and a matchstick or nail to get it out of holes. Never dry wet leather near a direct source of heat, or it will go brittle. Instead, try to let it dry naturally in a dry room that is comfortably warm, but not hot. When it's dry, apply a leather-conditioner.

Store tack in a room that doesn't get damp, or it will go mouldy. Recent mould growth can be removed with an anti-fungal product made for use on leather; as these tend to dry it out, you'll need to follow it with leather-conditioner.

Some of the best leather-conditioning products are in the form of balm or cream rather than oil. The problem with oils is that it's easy to apply too much, which weakens the fibres in the leather and leads to stretching.

Time-saving tips

For everyday use, boots and girths that can be hosed off save time and money. They can also prevent the spread of disease on yards where it may be impractical for every horse to have dedicated equipment, such as dealers' yards. Girths can be taken off one horse, dunked in an appropriate mild disinfectant solution, dried and used on another.

Girths that can be dunked in a mild disinfectant solution help prevent the spread of disease.

'Velvet-covered browbands are a nightmare to keep clean. We use them only on show bridles and make cotton covers with Velcro fastenings which stay in place until just before the horse goes in the ring.'
Lynn Russell

THOROUGH CLEANING

Unless you have limitless time – or someone to do it – life is too short to dismantle and clean tack thoroughly every day. However, it's essential to do this once a week and you'll find that the latest leather-care products make the process easier and quicker. Use this time as an opportunity to check tack for safety.

LEATHER

There are two steps to cleaning dismantled leather tack thoroughly: removing grease and dirt, then feeding the leather. Everyone has favourite methods and products, but this section might offer new ideas.

Traditionally, dirt is removed with plain water, and saddle soap is then applied. However, 'soap' is a misleading name, as it conditions rather than cleans, and if there are heavy grease deposits, water alone may not be enough if you are using a plain sponge.

Instead, try a face cloth or flannel, as textured fabric lifts dirt more efficiently. This is less messy than the traditional, but still effective, method of making a cleaning pad of mane or tail hair.

You may also want to use one of the new generation of leather cleaners, formulated to remove grease without damaging the leather.

Textured fabric lifts dirt.

Leather has grain (left) and flesh sides.

Leather has two sides, a grain (smooth) side that has been sealed during the manufacturing process and a flesh (rough) side that has open pores. Once you've cleaned leather, you need to feed it, concentrating on the flesh side, as this will absorb the leather food.

Glycerine saddle soap contains conditioners and is fine for routine use, but once a month, or more frequently if leather starts to become dry, you need to use a specialist product.

Good-quality leather tack that has had regular applications of glycerine saddle soap doesn't shine, but acquires a soft gleam. Boot polish gives a shine, but also makes leather slippery, so its use on tack cannot be recommended.

Leather food keeps tack supple.

> **TIP**
> Glycerine soap should be applied with a sponge that is barely damp, or it will foam up and be ineffective. Don't wet the sponge, or you'll never be able to wring it out sufficiently. Instead, apply a few drops of water to the bar and wipe a dry sponge over it. The grooms of yesteryear spat on their saddle soap, but nowadays, that probably isn't recommended Health and Safety procedure!

METALWORK

Bits and stirrup irons can be washed and then dried. If you dip them in hot, clean water for a final rinse, then immediately dry and polish them with a clean cloth, you'll get a pleasing shine.

Metal polish should be used sparingly, and never on bits, as you don't want any residue getting into your horse's mouth. If your browband has brass or metal decoration, the easiest way to get it clean and shiny is to apply polish on a cotton-wool bud.

Bits with a high copper content marketed under names such as Aurigan have an attractive golden tone when new, but this gradually dulls. If you want to restore the bling factor, buy special cleaning paste made especially for them.

Finally, although life is too short to clean tack every day, time spent cleaning it is never wasted. As this book has shown, tack makes a huge difference to your horse's comfort and performance. It's an investment, and as such should be looked after.

'To bring an "as-new" shine to stainless steel bits and stirrups, put them in the dishwasher.'
Malan Goddard, UK master saddler

QUESTIONS AND ANSWERS

Q I bought an expensive rug with straps that go round the horse's hind legs, but the straps are causing problems. They are rubbing the hair of my horse's legs and if I loosen them off, the rug slips. How can I prevent this happening?

A If your rug also has cross surcingles, the standard way of fastening rear legstraps is to link them. Take the left strap and pass it round the horse's hind leg, then clip it to the left-hand side of the rug. Next, take the right strap, pass it through the left one and round the horse's hind leg and clip to the right-hand side of the rug.

The straps should be adjusted so that you can fit a hand's width between each strap and the horse's legs, as shown here. However, if the straps form part of an underbelly harness, check with the manufacturer, as recommended adjustment methods vary.

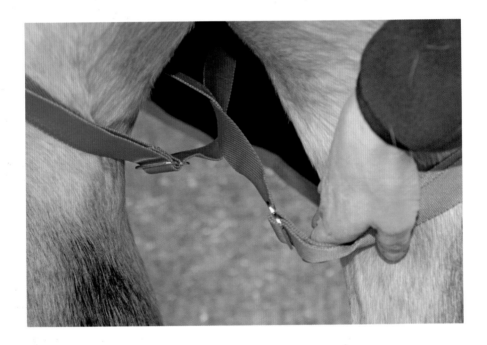

Q When I bought my horse, his previous owner also sold me his saddle. I've had it checked by my saddler, who says it's a good fit for him – but it's causing problems when we go on long rides and I find my hips ache. I didn't get this discomfort with my previous horse, so could the saddle be causing it?

A If the saddle twist (waist) doesn't suit your proportions, it can make riding uncomfortable or even painful. If it is too narrow, it will bring tears to your eyes and drastically affect your position. If it is too wide, you will feel that you are having to widen your pelvis and hips to an uncomfortable extent. Women tend to have more problems than men – don't feel embarrassed about talking to your saddle fitter, as he or she will be well aware of this problem and will be able to find you another saddle that suits you and your horse.

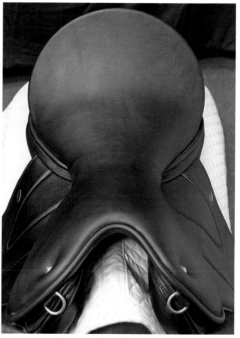

A saddle that fits your horse and has a twist to suit your proportions will be comfortable for both of you.

Q My horse has been diagnosed with arthritis and my vet has suggested that when he has to be stabled, I use stable bandages to give warmth and support. I sometimes have to ask staff at my livery yard to bring him in at night and the owner says she will have to charge for this, as it's so time-consuming and must be done by someone very experienced. Is there anything else I could do?

A Well-designed, padded stable boots such as the Kentaur ones (see page 143) are a good alternative to bandages. They are quicker to put on and it is unlikely that anyone could cause problems by fastening them too tightly. Your horse may also benefit from magnetic therapy – try a magnetic back pad (see page 172) or boots.

ACKNOWLEDGMENTS

The more you learn about horses, the more you realize there is to learn. One of the most difficult things is to decide on certain principles, but at the same time remain open-minded. Many experts have helped by sharing their knowledge and opinions for this book and while they may not agree with everything it contains, their input over the years is greatly valued.

They include Mark Fisher, Master Saddler and consultant to the British Equestrian Federation and World Horse Welfare (formerly the International League for the Protection of Horses); Kate Jerram, whose expertise in 'making' young horses includes detailed analysis of the tack that best suits them; Lynn Russell, who has a remarkable gift for spotting and bringing out potential in horses that many less gifted producers would let slip through their fingers; Carol Mailer, a show jumping trainer and inventor, and Heather Moffett, founder of Enlightened Equitation and a tireless innovator.

Finally, in true Oscars style, special thanks are due to my husband, John, who took the photographs for this book and spent hours working out not only how to show equipment clearly, but to demonstrate how it works. The photo session with double bridle bits suspended on nylon thread was particularly inventive.

USEFUL CONTACTS

The following websites may offer more information about tack and equipment featured in this book. The author and photographer would like to thank many of the companies below and also master saddler Mark Fisher of Woolcroft Equine Services, Mays Lane, Leverington, Wisbech, Cambs UK for help in sourcing items for photography.

David Ahn Suberpad
www.davidahnequine.co.uk

Albion
www.albionsaddlemakers.com

Barnsby
www.barnsby.com

Belstane Marketing
www.belstane.com

Dr Cook's Bitless Bridle
www.bitlessbridle.com

Laura Dempsey, side-saddle maker
www.lauradempseysaddler.com

Dress Circle Horsewear
www.dresscirclehorsewear.com

Equilibrium Products
www.equilibriumproducts.com

FALPro
www.falpro.com

Flair/WOW saddles
www.wowsaddles.com

Horseware
www.horseware.com

E Jeffries
www.ejeffries.co.uk

Kentaur
www.kentaur.cz

Libbys
www.libbys-tack.com

Claire Lilley
www.clairelilley.com

Pee Wee bit
www.peeweebit.com

Rockin S bit
www.rockinsqh.com and
www.bewithyourhorse.com

William Micklem (Rambo Micklem Multibridle)
www.WilliamMicklem.com

Myler bits
www.toklat.com

National Sweet Itch Helpline/Boett Blanket
www.sweet-itch.co.uk

Snuggy Hoods
www.snuggyhoods.com

Thermatex
www.valebrothers.co.uk

Thorowgood
www.thorowgood.com

Diana Thompson (sidepull bridles)
www.dianathompson.com

V-Bandz
www.v-bandz.co.uk

Veredus
www.zebraproducts.co.uk

Westropp
www.westropphorseboots.co.uk

Page references in italic indicate illustrations.